40

No Fixed Address

TALES OF A RELUCTANT SAILOR

The Bequia Bookshop Co. Ltd.
P. O. Box 11
Port Elizabeth, Bequia
784-458-3905

By

Heather Morgan

The Bequia Bookshop Co. Ltd.
P.O. Box 11
Port Elizabeth, Bequia
784-458-3905

No Fixed Address

No Fixed Address

TALES OF A RELUCTANT SAILOR

By

Heather Morgan

Printed in the United States of America
Illustrations by Nicolette Morgan
Book Design by Createspace

ISBN 10: 0615763995

EAN 13: 9780615763996

Library of Congress Control Number: 2013902162
CreateSpace Independent Publishing Platform
North Charleston, South Carolina

U.S. Copyright TXU1-818-031
www.daisyatsea.com

For Bob, Nicolette, Edward, Daniela, Mary, and Bill

Contents

Acknowledgments

When my husband, Bob, and I started this journey, we received tremendous support from our family and friends, despite their secretly believing we had lost our minds. Their help and encouragement made this book possible, and I remain indebted to them.

From the beginning of my life on board I kept a journal, which over time turned into a scrapbook with photographs and sketches. When my fun-loving friend, Angie Carl looked at the scrapbook and commented, "You really should publish this," I simply had to take her remark seriously. I thank you Angie for opening my eyes to this opportunity.

I would also like to give special thanks to my very dear friend Alan Jansen, who has steadfastly encouraged and supported me throughout this writing process.

I owe a huge debt of thanks to my fabulous copyeditor, Karen Parkin, for all her hard work in helping me bring this manuscript to life, and to Julie Klein, my proofreader.

I owe very special thanks to my wonderful children, Nicolette, Edward, and Daniela, who loved and supported me throughout this adventure, even though they secretly thought their Mother had lost her mind. I love you all immeasurably.

Nicolette's fabulous illustrations that depict scenes from my story, never cease to bring a smile to my face. I am blown away by her talent, and I'm so grateful for her humor (which helps me to always see the lighter side of life). Her illustrations can be seen on my website, www.daisyatsea.com

Words cannot express my gratitude for everything Edward does for me. For always making me laugh, and keeping my spirits up. For his positive, upbeat approach; unwavering support for my unconventional lifestyle; and constant encouragement for my writing.

I am so deeply indebted to Daniela, not only for encouraging my writing in innumerable ways but for taking on the considerable burden of managing everything on land for her father and me for almost five years, giving us the freedom to travel.

I would like to express heartfelt thanks to my father-in-law, Bill, who has always remained a faithful fan and a regular supporter and reader of my blog.

To my wonderful husband, Bob, 'my true north' (in every sense of the word), my gratitude is bittersweet. Our journeys aboard Daisy forced me frequently to face my greatest fear, but at the same time blessed me with the most amazing experiences imaginable. I can't envisage my life without the mind-blowing adventures we've shared together.

Finally to my adorable mother, Mary Osborne, who has been my rock, a steadfast pillar of support and encouragement to me in everything I've ever done with my life, even this crazy journey. Mum, there are not enough words to thank you for all you have done for me.

Introduction

This is my story of our five-year journey south, an island-hopping adventure that took us from Tortola in the British Virgin Islands, down the island chain as far as Grenada, then west through the islands off the Venezuelan coast, all the way to the exotic ABCs: Aruba, Bonaire, and Curacao.

This adventure started back in November 2006 when my husband, Bob, realized his lifelong dream of buying an Oyster sailboat. From his very first glimpse of one of these amazing sailboats, back in the early eighties, his dream had been born. No other boat would do, and owning an Oyster became his goal in life. And once Bob makes up his mind, it's as good as done. There was never a doubt in my mind that he would indeed own an Oyster sailboat one day.

Bob wasn't content to just *own* the boat: he wanted to live aboard permanently. And he convinced me to do it—I'm not even sure how. This proposed alternate lifestyle wasn't just a simple change of address. It meant selling my beautiful home, abandoning practicality and security, and leaving behind my beloved grown children, pets, horses, friends—everything dear to me. I'm still a little fuzzy about how it all came to fruition.

But once we decided to go forth with the plan, I demonstrated my full support by enrolling in a three-day basic sailing course in Miami, Florida. My twenty-five-year-old daughter, Nicolette, joined me on the course, and we both really enjoyed it. We sailed in a lovely bay, with perfect weather, on a thirty-six-foot sailboat. Even though our training boat was almost half of our own boat's length, the principles of sailing are the same, and it was a great opportunity for the two of us to get to grips with the basic skills necessary for a life aboard. I told myself any knowledge gained would be good because my hands-on sailing experience was extremely limited. Even after ten years of chartering in the Caribbean, my son, Edi, had always been with us and had done all the actual sailing with Bob, leaving me solely to galley duty. Having thoroughly enjoyed the sailing course with Nicolette and then surprising myself by passing the course exam with flying colors, my enthusiasm was growing. I told myself, "Maybe this isn't going to be so bad after all."

After sailing school, the next step toward our new life was to sell our home. This initiated one of the most stressful periods of our lives: We were exchanging our 12,000-square-foot home for a 58-foot yacht—a major lifestyle change, however you look at it. We would be leaving ourselves with no land base, no home to return to, and no fixed address.

The sale of our home took a lengthy eighteen months, due to the economic crash that occurred just as our house hit the market. As always, our timing had been less than perfect, but we didn't let this deter us. We used that time to travel to and fro between our home in Cincinnati and our sailboat *Crazy Daisy* (from this point on referred to simply as *Daisy*), which was situated in the beautiful islands of the Caribbean, specifically the British Virgin Islands.

Once the house was finally sold, we put all our possessions into storage and moved our youngest daughter, Daniela, into a townhouse near her school. Our other children, Nicolette and Edward, were already living away from home near their schools and work. With our family comfortably situated in their various locations, we were free at last to move permanently onto our dreamboat and set sail around the globe. Bob's dream had always been to do a circumnavigation, whereas I had imagined, or rather hoped, that we would use the boat simply for vacations, bobbing quietly around the Caribbean.

At this point I should mention that I am really the most unlikely sailor you'll ever meet: I'm absolutely terrified of deep water. A swimming pool accident when I was eight years old instilled in me a fear of water that has always held me back. Although I should add that my confidence with swimming improved immeasurably over the five years of living aboard. I still swim like a turtle, with my head held high above the water, and my hair rarely even gets wet, but at least I gained enough courage over the years to allow myself to swim off the boat without fear.

Considering my initial fear of deep water, it seems truly bizarre that I would have even considered moving onto one of those scary, floating confined spaces, where the very real probability of drowning is an everyday possibility. And yet I somehow allowed myself to be sucked into this madness. I was about to embark on a journey where I could lose sight of land for possibly days at a time. I would see nothing but water and be continually surrounded by alarmingly large, razor-toothed critters and slimy stingers that would be swarming in great numbers below *Daisy*, patiently waiting for me to trip up. This would, of course, initiate the dreaded man-overboard procedure and alert the ocean's enormous man-eaters, who would all be excitedly yelling to each other in fishy language: "dinner's served." Fortunately for me, we have not as yet had to deploy the man-overboard lifeline, life raft, or anything else, but that's not to say that I still don't live in perpetual fear of it.

What's more, there is nothing in my background to suggest that I was destined for a life at sea. Since I was very young, I've read about the great explorers and their amazing adventures, but I never once dreamed that I would do anything in my life remotely resembling any of the incredible adventures I had read about. I grew up in a typical middle class family in Bristol, England. My family didn't travel much. Dad was occupied by the family business he inherited. Mum helped him with the business but was otherwise a stay-at-home mum.

I was eighteen when I first started dating Bob, who was just sixteen. He was building a seventeen-foot sailboat in his dad's garage. We spent many nights in the garage working on the construction of the boat, sanding and varnishing till the early hours while our friends were out clubbing and having fun. I should have realized there and then that if I stayed with him I would one day end up on the water. But sailing was one of the few sports I had no intention of getting involved in. Oh, how wrong I was!

Throughout the years, I'd heard many stories of people who give up everything conventional and land-based to take to the sea, swapping earth for water, one might say. Despite ten years of chartering boats, my sailing experience was limited to the quiet waters around the British Virgin Islands. This does not constitute ocean sailing, which is quite different. My only actual oceangoing experiences were through television and books. My reading on the topic consisted of *117 Days Adrift*, *Pirates Aboard*, and *Godforsaken Sea*. Not surprisingly, none of this reading material had exactly filled me with the desire to throw caution to the wind, embrace a life at sea, and change my name along the way to Long Jane Silver.

As our departure date neared, the initial excitement and enthusiasm that I felt after sailing school was dwindling fast. I was starting to feel somewhat less than ecstatic at the prospect of making such a dramatic change in my comfortable life. But I had given my word. I had agreed. I couldn't back down now. This was Bob's chance to realize his dream and I couldn't take that away from him. I was committed (or maybe I should have been committed) to the dream.

So in November 2006, Bob and I launched our nautical adventure. As with all cruisers, we amassed a multitude of both amusing and horrific tales to tell during those early months aboard *Daisy*. The tragic tales were mostly mine, due to my total lack of expertise and experience, along with my extraordinary desire to demonstrate my amazing skills as a first mate. Sadly, as it happened, I discovered to my dismay that I did not possess skills of any kind when it came to sailing. But as it's said, one learns through errors, so I had high hopes of quickly becoming extremely well educated in all things nautical.

I have to admit, though, that living aboard has definitely heightened my appreciation for the smaller things in life, things that landlubbers take for granted, such as a well-stocked grocery store just around the corner; a loo that always flushes, doesn't flood, and doesn't constantly need to be dismantled and repaired (quite possibly the nastiest of boat chores); a dry and comfortable bed at night; and cereals, biscuits, and cookies that aren't soggy—just to name just a few.

Although I'm not the first person to write about travels throughout these islands, I have a unique take that I hope you'll find both helpful and humorous. You'll get an insider's perspective on boating and island life, useful facts and information on the islands, and some of my great boat-friendly recipes, using ingredients that are found in the Caribbean or easily stored in the boat galley—all punctuated with illustrations by my daughter, Nicolette Morgan, and photos I've taken along the way.

If you were to ask me if I would I do it again, my adrenaline would start pumping and with just a moment's hesitation, I would probably say yes. Even though I hate sailing, and I'm scared to death of deep water and bad weather, and I'm bored silly on long crossings, I just can't imagine my life without this adventure. I've been blessed with so many incredible experiences on this journey that I just had to share them. So here's my story, and I hope you enjoy it.

Chapter 1

Oh, for a Life at Sea

On a gorgeous, sunny afternoon in late November 2006, at the port of Red Hook, St. Thomas, we boarded our sailboat, *Daisy*, and set sail on our first adventure. The first eighteen months aboard were spent sailing around the Caribbean, mainly in the friendly waters of the British Virgin Islands (BVI) and up and down the east coast of America. Captain Bob was absolutely in his element, happily familiarizing himself with all the systems and workings of the boat. Meanwhile, I spent my time bouncing around a galley the size of a shoebox, attempting to prepare gourmet meals in sweltering heat. I had a lot of adjustments to make.

I quickly discovered that escapism comes with its costs (speaking as a sailor's wife who's somewhat reluctantly living aboard). This unusual life of mine had me feeling both blessed and cursed, depending entirely upon the unexpected circumstances that I frequently found myself in since adopting this bizarre and unorthodox lifestyle.

On the positive side, I was blessed with countless adventures, unlimited freedom, and the wonders of traveling to exotic locations. I met interesting people from all over the world, had the opportunity to learn about many different fascinating cultures, and increased my geographical knowledge.

A few of my everyday pastimes included climbing volcanoes; swimming with sharks, rays, and turtles; sailing with dolphins and whales; and hiking through screeching jungles, chasing monkeys and other wildlife, armed only with my

1

trusty camera. I went where I wanted, when I wanted, for as long as I wanted, dependent only upon the weather (and, of course, Captain Bob). I didn't wear a watch or worry about time. My days were measured in daylight and lasted from sunrise till sunset. I breathed clean, unpolluted air and ate fish fresh out of the ocean. I was perpetually windswept and sun-kissed. I waltzed around barefoot in colorful sarongs. I spent vast amounts of my time exploring places most folks can only read or dream about and many have not even heard of. It was a privileged life that I led on board. You could say it was a sort of suburban housewife's attempt to follow in Darwin's footsteps (or should I say wake).

We headed out on each and every new adventure with the fridges, freezer, and hammocks fully stocked, expectantly searching for new islands where we could swim or snorkel in the crystal clear, tepid turquoise waters. We explored the islands and relaxed on the white sandy beaches, sipped delicious cocktails out of coconut shells, and lazed around in hammocks strung from the ship's mast or between two palms on the beach.

It all sounds idyllic, wouldn't you agree? A truly spoiled, irresistibly romantic existence spent luxuriating in some of the world's most exotic locations. Or was it?

My early hopes and dreams of a carefree existence were quickly dashed by the actual realities of boat life. The wondrous moments *did* exist, but were, in fact, quite few and far between. I'm referring here to the time spent in between visits to the remote atolls of paradise. A huge amount of time was spent in boatyards and marinas, with no breeze and sometimes no power, so no air-conditioning. Working in swelteringly hot, dusty conditions. Maintaining, repairing, replacing, sanding, and varnishing. Scalding our feet on burning-hot decks that were painful to walk upon. Climbing into tight, awkward places, attempting to repair a burst hose or replace a pump, only to discover that my arm was about three inches too short and we had the wrong parts or equipment. Waiting for those urgently needed parts that were held up by customs for weeks, sometimes months, at a time, just because they can. And dealing with customs, knowing that we were completely at their mercy and, oh, how they loved it.

Oh, and how could I forget all the mosquitoes, fending them off by the thousands. Spraying ourselves liberally with dangerous chemicals that rarely worked in a vain attempt to stop them biting, chemicals that did goodness only knows what sort of damage to our bodies.

The bites were followed by hours, days, sometimes even weeks of itching, burning, and scratching, coupled with the inability to sleep because of the painful irritation caused by the bites and the heat.

The perpetually windswept hair, which sounds so romantic, in reality was just a tangled mess that I would have struggled to get a broom through most days, let alone a hairbrush. The sun-kissed face was really only a tan concealing blotchy, leathery skin that was actually under serious threat of developing skin cancer and made me look twenty years older.

I was almost always barefoot, so my feet had spread in the most unattractive fashion. When I tried to wear shoes again, I found that nothing fit. They don't make women's shoes wide enough for me. All was not lost, however: I still fit into and looked great in my sexy pink flippers.

For the majority of sailors, the hours and hours and hours spent at sea are quite magical. Captain Bob, for example, was in nautical heaven. Not so much, sadly, for yours truly: Without the distraction of dolphins and whales, I was usually either leaning over the side vomiting or so dreadfully bored all I could do was sleep. I found myself desperately scouring the horizon for the next destination and counting the minutes until we could drop anchor. And what was worse is that, as a passionate cook, I was unable to prepare food while underway. I didn't function well in a burning hot galley that moved and swayed, so for long crossings (unless Captain Bob took over galley duty) we were usually either starving or snacking on nuts and chips—not the best diet.

For Captain Bob it was all about the journey; for me it was all about the destination.

Having said that, let the journey begin.

Tortola to St. Maarten

Coordinates: 18 25'N 64 35'W

Tuesday, June 3, 2008

My son, Edward ("Edi"), and I boarded a tiny six-seat aircraft for a noisy and somewhat bumpy flight from San Juan, Puerto Rico, to the spectacular British Virgin Islands. I absolutely love to fly, so for me the flight was enjoyable. Not so for Edi. For him, the flight was a white-knuckle, hair-raising, nauseating experience. Even the startling beauty of the islands below failed to provide enough distraction to alleviate his distress. The stomach-knotting, teeth-clenching blind panic one feels when helplessly bouncing around in a metal box several thousand feet up in the air is a fear all too real, and Edi was not amused.

My cat, Nicho-San, was also somewhat put out. His fancy designer travel case, which seemed such a good idea when I bought it, suddenly appeared way too small for him: with his hair all stood on end, and his tail bushed out like a raccoon's. Nicho's turquoise blue eyes grew as large as saucers, and I couldn't ignore the piercing "I'm going to piss on your pillow" looks he was giving me. Siamese cats, my favorite feline, really know how to make their feelings understood. They're snobby, feisty little individuals, with the airs and graces of royalty, who regard their owners as staff. Siamese will accept only their own kind and treat the rest of the animal kingdom and humanity with an air of contempt. Despite their aloofness, they're widely known within the feline world as elegant creatures. Most sport glossy coats and abs of steel. Sadly, Nicho-San does not conform to the breed standard on all levels: being a little overweight, he appears to have an udder that swings like a pendulum as he runs. It's amusing to watch, but don't let him catch you laughing at him. Although he has failed miserably with the abs of steel, I try to console myself with the knowledge that at least he has a luxurious, shiny coat.

Our aircraft made its bumpy landing on Beef Island, Tortola. Edi and I were a little shaken but thankfully unscathed, sporting perhaps a few extra gray hairs and bitten nails. It suddenly felt strange to be back in the islands: I had just enjoyed a lovely five-week stay in Ohio with Edi and my daughter, Daniela. Now I needed to adjust to island life all over again.

The second the airplane door swung open, the searing Caribbean heat hit me like a slap in the face. The humidity frizzled my hair, and I felt rivers of sweat running down my back. I trudged across the blazing hot tarmac toward the airport terminal, praying the building would be air-conditioned. I slung my flight bag over one shoulder and Nicho-San in his designer travel bag, hissing and spitting venom, over the other. The act of walking, balancing the bags, and scratching the bites from the welcoming party of mosquitoes was proving quite a difficult task.

Once in the un-air-conditioned terminal, clearing customs involved a couple of hitches with the department of agriculture over Nicho-San's paperwork. (See Appendix 1: Traveling Abroad with Animals). I was directed to a back office to complete the paperwork. Although the officer was pleasant and quite helpful, I couldn't help but wonder how much my low-cut tank top aided in his obvious distraction with the completion of the forms. I self-consciously tugged at my straps and tried unsuccessfully to cover myself, while he openly ogled my breasts in a way that made me want to reach across the desk and slap him. That probably wouldn't have ended well, so I restrained myself and tried to concentrate on the task at hand: completing Nicho-San's entry paperwork. Once it was all in order,

I bolted back to the terminal to help Edi collect the luggage, which had arrived on a different plane. We (OK, I) had brought so much luggage, the airline probably had to fly another plane behind ours just to transport it. We headed outside to our rental car and set off on the thirty-minute drive across the island to Road Town to pick up Bob, who had ferried over from St. Thomas.

We stuffed Bob's luggage into the little rental car, which was already nearly filled to capacity with my cases. I then dumped Nicho on Edi's lap and wedged myself between all the luggage in the backseat. Off we drove, doing a very plausible impersonation of "elephants in a mini" for the short drive out to Hodges Marina, where our boat, *Crazy Daisy*, was alongside waiting for us. Seriously, how apt is that name for our boat?

Images of the actress Anne Heche in the movie *Six Days and Seven Nights* sprang to mind as we drove along and I struggled for breath under the heaps of boxes, boat parts, bags, and cases. There's a great scene in that movie when they're marooned on an island and Anne Heche climbs into the back of the plane and accidently inflates the life raft. She finds herself squished in the back with her face pressed up against the window, practically unable to move except to raise her hand and give Harrison Ford the finger. I love that scene; unfortunately, I now felt as though I were imitating it.

With the nightmare trip behind us, we arrived at the marina—crinkled, creased, and quite exhausted. We were then faced with the monumental task of unpacking and stowing. This was not an easy procedure as once again, true to form, I'd arrived with more luggage than a small army. Being the Mother of Clutter and having failed miserably to conquer my compulsion to carry everything I might need with me in the event of a crisis, I realized too late that I had hauled along way too many belongings. Living on a boat requires a minimalistic lifestyle, a concept that I continue to struggle with.

Stowing took us awhile and involved quite a bit of sweating and cursing, as I managed to fill every conceivable space and then some, much to Bob's chagrin. It appeared that *Daisy* sank another six inches under the extra weight. After what felt like days of unpacking, fatigue and hunger claimed us. We walked to a little restaurant, perched in the most idyllic coastal setting just a few minutes from the marina. We enjoyed a good bottle of wine and an absolutely delicious dinner, and were then ready for a good night's sleep. I woke up early the next morning to complete the provisioning for the trip and return the rental car. That afternoon we motored quietly away from Hodges and sailed across to Cooper Island where we picked up a mooring for the night.

Cooper Island (18.3859 N 64.5118 W) is just one of an archipelago of over sixty islands that make up the incredibly beautiful British Virgin Islands.

Nicho-San on Deck, in Tortola.

The next morning (June 5) we enjoyed a sail up to the Bitter End resort on the island of Virgin Gorda, where we spent the rest of the day making the final preparations for our departure. The weather was typically fabulous for the Caribbean, and fortunately there was nothing predicted in the forecast to cause any concern. We anticipated clear skies, light to moderate winds, and calm seas—near perfect conditions for our sail across to St. Maarten.

Virgin Gorda (18 28'54.8"N 64 23'20.95"W) is the third-largest island in the BVI and another great place to visit. Christopher Columbus named the island the "Fat Virgin" because the island's profile on the horizon looks like a fat lady lying on her side.

We cast off shortly before 7 p.m., leaving Bitter End, forty-five degrees north of Necker Island, and headed out during a perfect Caribbean sunset. As so often is the case headed in that direction, the sail across to St. Maarten was quite rough, with an unwelcomed headwind for the entire leg. *Daisy* literally slammed up and down through the waves while rolling from side to side like a drunk.

After five weeks on land, my sea legs had totally deserted me, so I was consequently suffering from a major bout of seasickness. To add to the drama, poor Nicho-San, barely having recovered from his traumatic experience of bouncing around in the heavens, now found himself bouncing around on the ocean. He was barfing for all he was worth down below. I knew beyond a shadow of a doubt that he was going to piss on my pillow as soon as this nightmare trip was over. The horribly uncomfortable journey dragged on and on. Because of the headwind, we couldn't raise the sails, which would have steadied the boat. So we were forced to continue under motor. To those unfamiliar with sailing, I would relate this experience to a ride in one of those spinning teacups at the fairground, on full speed with a broken wheel while soaking wet!

A night crossing, with a calm sea and wind in the right direction, can be a truly peaceful and exhilarating experience. Night sailing is also the best time to fully appreciate the extraordinary beauty of the stars without the distraction of light from the mainland. As *Daisy* slices gracefully through the waves, hopefully the right way up, millions of luminous lights (bioluminescent) sparkle in the wake all around us. It's quite magical to witness. And I love watching the rising sun as it creeps over the horizon at dawn, its rays piercing the clouds with blinding planks of crimson and orange that cast shimmering lights over the water. Although I should add that after the chills of darkness, finally seeing daylight once again always brings mind-blowing relief for me. I especially love the first glimpse of new land as it appears magically through the distant mist. I always breathe a sigh of relief and offer up a silent prayer of thanks: land at last.

Although it's plainly obvious by now that there's really not anything of a natural sailor in my blood, I still manage to find deep inside me the willpower and love of travel that, despite my nervousness, lure me back (not forgetting, of course, that I have no choice, with my house being sold and all). An insatiable desire to travel farther and visit out-of-the way places unattainable to most folk is what really sets sailing apart from any other form of travel. Who the hell am I trying to convince here? Seriously!

When you sail, there are few limits to where you can go, and distance is no problem. With the wind as your power, sailing is actually an environmentally friendly form of travel; how could you improve on that? (Did I actually say that?)

Unfortunately for Nicho-San and me, this nighttime sail to St. Maarten wasn't one of those magical, peaceful crossings. But then again, in sailing, as in all things, one must learn to take the good with the bad. I'm still working on that.

Chapter 2

St. Maarten to St. Eustatius

Coordinates: St. Maarten 18 04'N 63 03'W, St. Eustatius 17 29"N 62 59'W

Friday, June 6

At 8 a.m. we dropped anchor in Simpson Bay, just outside the bridge at St. Maarten. It was another typically beautiful, sunny Caribbean morning. Just a hint of a light breeze swept the blissfully calm, quiet bay, which was a welcome change after the roller coaster of a sail from the night before. Bob, Edi, and I sat on deck under the shade of the bimini, enjoying a delicious breakfast of scrambled eggs, smoked salmon, and steaming hot coffee. Edi was making me laugh as usual with his hilarious impersonation of Inspector Clouseau (from the movie *The Pink Panther*). Yes, all was well with the world: the nightmare leg from Virgin Gorda was behind us, and we had our appetites back.

For so many reasons I love having my children on board. All three are far more competent sailors than I. Danni is incredibly observant. Nic brings both competency and humor to the mix, which is so welcome during times of stress (and there's usually quite a bit of stress aboard a ship, particularly *Crazy Daisy*). And Edi has saved me from my messy blunders more times than I can count.

Edi at the helm

There was just one unfortunate time a couple of years ago when Edi was a little too late to prevent one of my many faux pas. We were moored in Honeymoon Bay, St. John, getting ready to set sail. Edi and Captain Bob were busy at the helm, so I offered to cast off. "Sure you know how to do it?" Captain Bob asked. "I think so," I replied. "You just have to untie the line from the mooring ball and let it go. Signal me when we're off, OK?" he said. "No problem," I replied. This would be the first time I was to cast off. Edi had always done it in the past. I was trying to learn because soon I would be doing all the first-mate jobs Edi had been doing until now; he was due to fly back to the States in a few short weeks.

I made my way up to the bow, untied the line, and let it go. I waved to Bob and Edi back at the helm. "We're off," I shouted. I walked back to the cockpit smiling, feeling very proud of myself. That wasn't at all difficult, I thought. We were heading out of the bay when Ed turned to me and said, "Did you put the line back in the anchor locker?" I looked at him dumbfounded. "Line, you mean the line that was tied to the mooring ball?" Edi's eyebrows shot up. "Yes," he replied. But his expression said, "Oh crap, what's she done?" I started to feel uneasy.

"I did exactly what you said, I untied it and let it go," I shot back, knowing then that I was in trouble again. "You let it go? Oh crap, crap, crap," was all he could say as he turned to tell Captain Bob the bad news. "We need to go back."

My mediocrity as first mate now totally confirmed, all I could do was apologize. "I'm so sorry, I thought it was part of the mooring ball—you didn't say untie it and bring it on board!"

Bob turned Daisy around and we made our way back to the mooring ball. I fervently hoped the line would still be attached so we could retrieve it. I sat quietly in the cockpit, feeling really dumb. When I thought about it, I realized it was quite obvious that the line was ours. My trouble has always been that I tend to act before I think; it's something I've been guilty of my whole life. But I was really going to have to make a change if I was to survive a life at sea. This was not a comforting thought.

Another important first-mate responsibility was operating the mainsail, preferably without jamming up the hydraulics and tearing a hole in the sail. Yes, I actually did that, too. Sometimes I panicked under pressure, and half the jobs I had to do on board scared me senseless.

I also discovered to everyone's horror (and amusement) that I was totally inept at driving our dinghy, *Whoops-a-Daisy*, displaying nothing resembling control. I'm sure I put the fear of God into the hearts of the other boat occupants unfortunate enough to be in the harbor at the same time as I—at least those within range who were close enough to witness my acts of incompetent lunacy.

One unfortunate dinghy-driving incident was the last straw for Captain Bob. I almost turned *Whoops-a-Daisy* upside down by hitting forward instead of reverse and driving it at full throttle up over *Daisy*'s stern. My poor husband felt that the only safe option—before I killed either myself or some other poor innocent who happened to be in my way—was to have a steering wheel fitted. This would hopefully give me some semblance of control and perhaps increase my life expectancy.

The line was gone when we got back to the mooring ball. Oh well, I thought, this just has to be chalked up as another lesson learned—something to add to my long and amusing list of misadventures at sea.

Anyway, I digress: back to my musings about St. Maarten.

St. Maarten is the smallest island in the world to have been partitioned between two different nations, which created a unique cultural mix. The island has been shared by the French and the Dutch for almost 350 years.

During one of my visits to St Maarten, I heard of an amusing legend that tells of the original partitioning of the island. Two men, one from each nation a Frenchman, and a Dutchman were to walk in opposite directions around the island, starting at Oyster Pond and meeting at the other side of the island. The crafty Frenchman, however, gave the Dutchman a bottle of gin and a bottle of wine before they parted. So the Dutchman, having drunk the booze on his walk, didn't make it any further than Cupecoy Bay. As agreed, the imaginary line between that beach and Oyster Pond was drawn to constitute the border. Consequently, the French got the largest part of the 33.5-square-mile island, and the Dutch only 13 square miles.

We were so content relaxing and basking in the early morning sun—chatting and enjoying our breakfast and coffee—that we totally missed the 9:30 a.m. bridge opening. The bridge wasn't due to open for incoming traffic again until 11:30 a.m., so we decided to skip St. Maarten altogether and move on. (We had only planned on spending a few hours in St. Maarten anyway, and the $60 bridge fee and $40 harbor fee seemed a lot to spend for a short visit.)

Our next important decision was determining which island to visit next. It was a toss-up between St. Barts and St. Eustatius. Because we had visited St. Barts many times, we agreed to check out the little island of St. Eustatius, affectionately called "Statia" by the locals.

We had an easy sail over and arrived in Oranjestad Bay by midafternoon. Statia, part of the Dutch Antilles, is a peaceful little island with about 3,500 inhabitants. Rumor has it that very few tourists make the effort to visit this lovely little, off-the-beaten-path Dutch island. This is a real shame because St. Eustacia is most definitely worthy of investigation. There are no spectacular beaches and very few shops, but it more than makes up for that with its dramatic and colorful scenery. The island offers an array of attractions for hikers and divers, but if these two sports don't interest you, you won't find a lot to do here. Culturally, Statia is a world away from St. Maarten and St. Barts.

Statia was once a thriving island that prospered from the slave trade in the eighteenth century but then lost everything in the nineteenth century with the abolition of slavery. A museum, located right in the center of the tiny island's only town, Oranjestad, chronicles the island's complex and troubled history. There are many abandoned warehouses and ruins in Oranjestad, but they are steadfastly being renovated into hotels and restaurants as the island endeavors to develop its tourist industry. Oranjestad is also working toward becoming a UNESCO World Heritage Site.

We admired the seafront properties, mostly pretty little gingerbread houses colorfully painted in typical Caribbean style. Gardens with white picket fences burst with brightly colored bougainvillea, hibiscus, oleander, frangipani, lush green palms, and flowering fauna. Geckos raced across the ground in all directions, and mother hens strutted about followed with military precision by lines of baby chicks. Magnificent flamboyant trees lined the sides of the road and grew wild on the hillsides, creating a painter's palette of vibrant red and green. Hummingbirds zipped from flower to flower. An atmosphere of beauty and tranquility surrounded us. This lovely little island truly is far from the fast-paced city life.

Statia's spectacular underwater reefs are quite possibly one of the Caribbean's best-kept secrets. I've heard tell that the diving there is really wonderful, although Statia has yet to achieve a reputation for its diving possibilities. The islanders proudly tell of their fabulous virgin reefs, alive with an abundance of fish and amazing colorful coral and underwater plant life. There are many sea turtles; and numerous historical shipwrecks. Statia has over thirty dive sites marked with buoys, mostly located in the south and north-west, where fishing and anchoring is prohibited. If you go, you should know that diving here is permitted only through local dive operators. Divers are asked to contribute to the marine parks maintenance by purchasing a dive tag.

For hikers, Statia boasts a dormant volcano called the Quill, which has a lush rain forest center. There are some really great hiking trails from the west side of town that wind up the slopes of the volcano to the edge of the crater. From the top, you can descend into the crater to the rain forest growing within.

Me with the cannon Ed wanted to take back to Daisy!

After our island exploration, we stopped for cocktails at a small hotel over-looking the ocean. Captain Bob was able to connect to the Internet to check on the weather for the next few days; meanwhile, Edi and I kicked back, sipping margaritas and rum punch cocktails and watching the sunset. Soon we were back on the boat, and I prepared dinner.

We ate dinner on deck that night, enjoying the warm, gentle breezes under a star-filled, cloudless sky. With a good bottle of wine, delicious food, and great conversation, our evening couldn't have been better. One of the many advantages of a sailing vacation is that everyone is together. Some of the happiest times in my life have been spent on board with my family. That night we all slept the sleep of the dead, as *Daisy* gently rocked and rolled in the bay.

Scrambled Eggs with Smoked Salmon

3 tablespoons ice-cold unsalted butter, diced
½ red bell pepper, seeded and diced (set some aside for the garnish)
8 large free-range eggs
3 tablespoons heavy cream
Sea salt and freshly ground black pepper
Small bunch of cilantro, chopped
¼ pound smoked salmon, shredded
4 English muffins, sliced in half and lightly toasted
8 pitted black olives

1. Preheat the oven to 250 degrees F.
2. Melt 1 tablespoon butter in a medium-size nonstick pan over medium heat.
3. Add most of the diced pepper and cook and stir for about 5 minutes, just enough to soften the peppers. Remove the peppers from the pan and drain on a kitchen paper towel. Place the peppers in an ovenproof dish and keep them warm in the oven while you make the eggs.
4. Break the eggs into a bowl and beat with a whisk to combine yolks and whites.
5. Add the heavy cream and peppers to the eggs and pour the mixture into a clean, cold nonstick pan. Gently cook on low heat.
6. Add 2 tablespoons butter, stirring frequently. As the mixture begins to set, add the remaining butter. The eggs will take about 5 to 6 minutes to scramble. Don't let them get too hot, or they will start to overcook and dry out. Keep moving the pan on and off the heat. Season the eggs with salt and pepper at the last minute.
7. Gently stir the chopped cilantro and smoked salmon into the scrambled eggs.
8. Serve immediately on the toasted muffins and garnish with olives and the remaining chopped peppers.
   Enjoy.

Coconut Rice with Mango

2 tablespoons unsalted butter
2 cups uncooked jasmine rice
1 tablespoon molasses
½ teaspoon sea salt
2 cups water
1 (14-ounce) can unsweetened coconut milk
1 ripe mango, peeled and diced small
1 tablespoon salted peanuts, crushed (optional)
1 tablespoon cilantro, chopped, for garnish

1. Melt the butter in a large saucepan over medium heat. Add the rice and stir well to coat with the butter. Stir in the molasses and salt; immediately add the water and coconut milk. Bring to a boil; reduce heat to low. Cover the saucepan and simmer gently for about 20 minutes, until the liquid is absorbed.
2. Remove the saucepan from the heat. With a fork separate and fluff the rice; stir in the diced mango. Place a paper kitchen towel over the pan and re-cover the pan with the lid. Let it stand for 5 minutes before serving. Garnish with the chopped peanuts and cilantro.

Enjoy.

Lemon Cream with Strawberry Shots

Lemon Cream:

4 large free-range eggs
⅓ cup plus 1 tablespoon confectioners' sugar
Juice and zest of 4 lemons
4 sheets gelatin, soaked in water
⅓ cup fine sugar

Strawberry Shots:

Juice and zest of 1 orange
⅓ cup Cointreau liqueur
2 cups fresh strawberries, hulled and quartered

1. Separate the eggs, putting the whites and yolks in different bowls.
   Whisk the egg yolks with ⅓ cup confectioners' sugar and the lemon zest until thick and creamy. Squeeze out the gelatin sheets and warm gently in the lemon juice until dissolved; stir into the egg yolk mixture.
2. Whisk the egg whites and fine sugar until stiff peaks form, then fold the mixture into the egg yolk mix. Pour the mix into four individual serving glasses and refrigerate for at least 2 hours.
3. In a medium bowl, mix the orange juice, orange zest, and Cointreau. Add the strawberries, stir well, and refrigerate for a minimum of 1 hour.
4. Put the chilled strawberry mix into a blender and blend to a smooth liquid. Strain the liquid through a fine sieve to remove the seeds; pour the mix into individual shot glasses.

   To serve: Sift 1 tablespoon confectioners' sugar over the lemon creams and serve with the shot glasses alongside.

   Note: This recipe includes raw eggs.
   Enjoy.

[Cook's note]

I always like to make my own curry paste: it's consistently so much better than the ready-made versions sold in a jar, which always taste really bland and a little funky to me. If you don't have the time or the ingredients, however, a ready-made curry sauce will have to do—just add some extra lime juice and a splash of fish sauce and you're good to go. You can adjust the heat by reducing the number of jalapenos. My family likes their food hot and spicy.

Daisy's Hot Curry Sauce

4 jalapenos, seeded and chopped
2-inch piece fresh ginger, peeled and chopped
4 to 6 cloves garlic, peeled
1 tablespoon cumin seed, coarsely ground
1 tablespoon coriander seed, coarsely ground
Grated zest of 1 large lime, plus about 2 tablespoons juice from the lime
1 teaspoon fish sauce
⅔ cup (approximately) light coconut milk
Sea salt and freshly ground black pepper

Put all the ingredients into a blender, blend to a paste, then pour into a small saucepan and simmer over a low heat for about 10 minutes.
Note: The curry sauce will keep in an airtight jar in the refrigerator for up to a week. Enjoy.

Grilled Swordfish

1 tablespoon olive oil
4 swordfish steaks, about 4 to 6 ounces each, cut about 1-inch thick
Sea salt and freshly ground pepper

1. Brush the olive oil over the swordfish steaks and season with salt and pepper.
2. Heat a sauté pan to medium high. When hot, add the swordfish and cook for about 3 to 4 minutes per side.
3. Test by peeking into the center of the steaks with the tip of a sharp knife. The fish should be tender, juicy, and opaque. Cover with foil and set aside until ready to serve. (As with most fish, undercooking is preferable to overcooking.)
   Serve with Daisy's Hot Curry Sauce and Coconut Rice with Mango.
   Enjoy.

[Cook's note]

For those of you who may not be curry lovers, I've included this as an alternative recipe for swordfish. It's equally delicious but without all the spices.

Grilled Swordfish with Peppers and Pine Nuts

¼ cup olive oil
6 swordfish steaks, about 4 to 6 ounces each, cut 1-inch thick
Salt and freshly ground black pepper
¼ pound (1 stick) salted butter
2 tablespoons capers
1 yellow bell pepper, seeded and diced
3 scallions, white and green parts, chopped
2 tablespoons pine nuts, toasted
2 tablespoons fresh tarragon leaves, roughly chopped
Juice and zest of 1 lemon

1. Brush the olive oil over the swordfish and season with salt and pepper.
2. Heat a sauté pan to medium high. When hot, add the swordfish and cook for about 3 to 4 minutes per side. Test by peeking into the center of the steaks with the tip of a sharp knife. The fish should be tender, juicy, and opaque. Cover with foil and set aside.

    (As with most fish, undercooking is preferable to overcooking.)
3. Melt the butter in a sauté pan until it turns a golden brown. Do not let the butter burn. Add the pepper and scallions; sauté for about 5 minutes. Add the pine nuts and tarragon, stir; add the capers, lemon juice, and zest. Spoon over the steaks and serve immediately.

    Enjoy.

Chapter 3

St. Eustatius to St. Kitts and Nevis

Coordinates: St. Kitts and Nevis 17 18'N 62 44W

Saturday, June 7

We weighed anchor at 10:30 a.m., and the gods must have been smiling upon us: the sail across from St. Eustatius to St. Kitts was absolutely lovely, with moderate 12- to 15-knot winds and calm seas—calm enough for me to actually enjoy the crossing.

As we approached the island in the late afternoon, I was enchanted. It was as though a little slice of the beautiful English countryside had been dropped right there into the middle of the cerulean blue ocean. Herds of cattle and sheep peacefully grazed in the lush green fields. Pretty little cottages and farms were scattered on the hillsides, and the flamboyant trees' brilliant red splashes punctuated the emerald green fields. It was reminiscent of my home country, with the exception of the flamboyant trees. Edi and I brought in the sails as we motored around to Porte Zante, where we had reserved a slip for the next couple of nights.

Coming alongside at Porte Zante and getting *Daisy* into the slip wasn't quite the calm and easy procedure we had hoped for. As we pulled into the somewhat confined space of the little harbor, we were confronted with a couple of large, rather cumbersome catamarans, maneuvering around with an apparent lack of control. Intelligently I feel, we hung back, giving the catamarans plenty of time and room to complete their clumsy attempts at docking. Well, at least I think they were trying to dock. They may have been trying to leave. We couldn't be sure what the hell they were attempting to do, so we kept *Daisy* well out of harm's way.

I'm constantly amused by the antics of some holidaymakers on charter boats. Most of them try to be captain, but all too few of them actually know what they're doing or even *why* they're doing it. There's really only room for one captain on any boat, no matter the size of the vessel. Between husband and wife, choosing a captain is often an ongoing battle, which frequently leads to many heated discussions. Most commonly it's the wives who stand proudly on the bow of the boat. They wave the boat hook around like Boadicea on her chariot, giving the most appalling directions to the poor person back at the helm, usually the husband, who frequently appears red faced and flustered as he attempts to maneuver the cat as he would his car in a parking lot.

Over the years, my observation of the unsuspecting boating community has provided me with endless entertainment—and writing material. Both experienced and novice boaters have found themselves in awkward and embarrassing situations through either negligence or just plain stupidity. I would hasten to add, however, that I'm easily as guilty as the next person when it comes to daft actions. I've made more than my fair share of careless blunders—most performed before an audience—that demonstrate my appalling mediocrity as a sailor and first mate. I've provided other boaters with sidesplitting entertainment at my expense. So I always feel at least a modicum of compassion when I see people being downright ridiculous in front of an audience. I'm constantly reminding myself that you learn from your mistakes, which actually means I should be bloody brilliant!

(For example, even after all these years of sailing, I am still perfecting many of the necessary nautical skills, such as maneuvering around the decks at speed without breaking my toes or knocking myself or other crewmembers over the side. I live in constant fear of initiating the man-overboard procedure and pray that we never have to.)

Anyway, back to Porte Zante: We were finally able to come alongside with the help of Bill and Heidi, who had a yacht on the neighboring slip. Like us, they were also steadily making their way down the island chain to Grenada and were kind enough to step in and give us a hand at docking. Once we secured all the lines and settled *Daisy* safely into her slip, we relaxed. A man appeared on the dock and introduced himself as Juni, a local taxi driver. He offered to take us on a tour of the island, which was something we had been planning to do. After haggling over the price for much longer than I considered proper, an agreement was reached. We arranged for Juni to pick us up at 9 a.m. the next morning.

Bill and Heidi invited us for a drink aboard their yacht, where we met Mr. Smee, their friendly little parrot who happily sat on my shoulder and pulled my hair while Edi took some photos.

Me and Mr Smee

We enjoyed some local beer and lively conversation with our new friends and neighbors. Then Heidi and I headed off to do a little shopping in the town, leaving the boys to their beer. To our dismay, every shop except the local supermarket was closed. We picked up a couple of groceries, and I almost had a coronary over the prices. I was in the middle of a heated conversation with the poor checkout girl over a bag of shrimp, when Heidi intervened and explained that the dollars were Caribbean, not American. Feeling rather stupid,

I apologized to the poor confused girl, paid my bill, and made a hasty retreat back to the dock.

That evening I was feeling the first symptoms of a cold with a scratchy throat, tight chest, and a slight fever. Bob and Edi picked up local Chinese takeout for dinner because I really didn't feel up to cooking. I retired to bed early with a book and a steaming hot cup of ginger, lemon, and honey tea, a comforting concoction my mother always made when any of us showed symptoms of a cold.

Sunday, June 8

The hot tea obviously worked its magic because the next morning I was feeling much better. Our taxi driver and tour guide, Juni, arrived bang on time at 9 a.m., and we set off on our tour of St. Kitts, a 68-square-mile island.

We drove out through Basseterre, the island capital, stopping along the way to take photographs. Juni gave us the history of the island and pointed out the important and historic buildings. The pride he felt for his island was touchingly evident.

Me, Captain Bob and Edi at Bloody Point, St.Kitts.

It was a scorching hot day as we continued our journey out through the local villages, following the coastline around the island. Lines of colorful washing hung outside every brightly painted house. Cattle, goats, sheep, and donkeys freely roamed about. We drove past several old abandoned sugar plantations. There are many dilapidated building remains that are little by little crumbling back to nature and slowly being reclaimed by the land. All the ruins were covered with colorful flora and fauna.

St. Kitts was once the wealthiest island in the Caribbean because of the sugar and tobacco that it produced. However, over the years the growing competition from larger countries has forced the sugar and tobacco growers to close their plantations one by one, as they could no longer compete. Today most of the old sugarcane fields lie neglected, growing uncontrolled and wild throughout the island. It didn't make sense to me that the fields weren't being farmed, as the soil is obviously fertile.

Like so many of the Caribbean islands today, St. Kitts thrives on tourism. The many cruise ships that stop here provide a welcome income for the islanders. The little town of Basseterre is quickly developing around catering to visiting tourists from the cruise liners. A whole new shopping center has sprung up at the port, with modern buildings and many up-market stores selling the usual high-priced artifacts, jewelry, and other touristy paraphernalia totally unrelated to the island or its history but, for reasons unfathomable to me, always in great demand by visitors. There were no cruise ships docked when we were there, so the town of Basseterre was very quiet.

Juni drove us inland to visit an old abandoned sugar plantation. A local boy approached us, and for a few dollars he proudly gave us an informed history of the plantation. The ruins, set at the foot of the rain forest, were breathtakingly beautiful. More cattle and goats roamed the ruins. Colorful hummingbirds flew overhead, feeding on the wild crimson, yellow, and pink hibiscus and other tropical flowers that grew everywhere in unrestrained profusion.

From the ruins, we drove up to the botanical gardens, which were bursting with more rich, lush green foliage and magnificent old flamboyant, breadfruit, mango, coconut palm, white cedar, and soursop trees. Everywhere we looked there were exotic tropical flowers, including amazingly delicate orchids. The vibrant array of colors and patterns were just incredible, the scent from the flowers intoxicating. Manmade balconies were perched high in the grounds, providing a welcome platform from which to overlook the lush rain forest surrounding the gardens. Dozens of dazzling butterflies hovered overhead, flitting from flower to flower. I made several attempts to photograph them, but they were too quick for me and I ended up with snapshots of colorful blurs.

We picked mangos from the trees and ate them. They were warm from the sun and sticky, but incredibly sweet and delicious. My camera was working overtime as I attempted to capture nature at its most glorious. My thoughts turned to my mum back in England. She had visited this island on a cruise a few years earlier, and I couldn't help thinking how much she would have enjoyed these gorgeous gardens. Had it not been for the intense heat, I could have happily stayed in the gardens all day. But I was beginning to feel like my skin was melting, so I made a hasty retreat back to our air-conditioned car.

Our next stop was the fort at Brimstone Hill, which dates from 1690 and is surrounded by cannons that were brought there by the British. The fort is currently being painstakingly restored by a local nonprofit organization. We spent a couple of hours exploring the ruins and stopping to admire the breathtaking panoramic views of the ocean, with the two peaks of Statia and Saba in the distance to the northwest, and then behind us the interior's lush green rain forest.

We managed to spot a couple of green monkeys (also called vervet monkeys) scampering around. They're said to outnumber humans two to one on the island, and they get up to all sorts of mischief. If you're touring the island, you're sure to see green monkeys as well as mongoose, which seem to appear everywhere.

When we left the fort, we drove down the other side of the island where we came across the luxurious new Marriott resort, which was surrounded by elaborate, expensive houses and fabulous villas perched high on the cliffs overlooking the bay. The Marriot boasts a beautiful bay, a golf course, and immaculately manicured lawns and gardens. We stopped for lunch at the very popular Shiggedy Shack on Frigate Bay's beach before returning home to *Daisy*.

I've heard it said that there's nothing much to see on St. Kitts. Whoever said that obviously hasn't explored the island. In my opinion, this island has a great deal to offer and should not be missed.

Monday, June 9

Still alongside at Porte Zante. We filled the water tanks and made *Daisy* ready for sail. I walked into town for a last-minute shop. I discovered an adorable little gift shop in the center of the town of Basseterre, away from the new shopping center, filled with genuine island-made goods—real souvenirs, not the imported stuff commonly found in touristy stores. I found some authentic St. Kitts gifts: locally embroidered clothing, table wear and cushions; brightly painted handmade pottery and wooden toys; and some lovely paintings by local artists—nothing factory produced, all manufactured and created here on the island. I bought some embroidered cushion covers for the salon and gifts for Nicolette and Daniela. Then I enjoyed a walk around the little town of Basseterre. By now I was getting hungry, so for lunch I bought a rotisserie chicken in one of the local stores and made a hasty return to the boat, eager to make my Caribbean-spiced chicken. My "happy with my purchases smile" faded as I attempted (but failed) to sneak all my shopping bags back on board: there was Captain Bob, greeting me with an "oh no, more stuff" look. Much to Bob's chagrin, I'm an avid collector of useless stuff, which will someday probably require us to upgrade from a fifty-eight-foot boat to a seventy-two-footer.

Back on board, I set about making lunch while Bob made a conference call for work and Edi took a nap with Nicho-San curled up on his lap.

By late afternoon, after a delicious lunch and a lazy nap, we were all well rested and ready to set off again. With steady 15-knot winds and calm seas, we had a very pleasant but short sail across to Nevis, arriving at about 5 p.m. We picked up a mooring off Pinney's Beach.

Pinney's Beach is reputed to be not only the most beautiful beach on Nevis but also one of the best beaches throughout the whole Caribbean. With its 4 miles of soft, golden sand; clear, calm water; and plenty of tall coconut palms offering welcome shade from the blistering sun, this is definitely a beach not to be missed. The Four Seasons loved it enough to build a high-end resort here. Although, it's funny: Whenever I read about a beach in the Caribbean, almost every island boasts of having the most beautiful beach. Really, I've seen a zillion Caribbean beaches, and the majority, if kept clean, are beautiful. I've yet to discover what actually constitutes one being the best.

As soon as *Daisy* was secure, we took *Whoops-a-Daisy* ashore for cocktails at the Four Seasons. We were directed to an outside table in the beautiful gardens overlooking the ocean. The view was spectacular! We lingered longer than we had initially intended, enjoying the scenery and cocktails served by our very attentive waiter. One would definitely not lack attentive service when staying here. A quick glance over the fabulous dinner menu almost convinced us to stay; however, we decided to return to *Daisy* because I already had our dinner planned.

For dinner I made Thai Spiced Salmon and Crispy Seaweed, which is a real crowd-pleaser. I've never served it to anyone who didn't absolutely love it. Everybody begs me for the recipe. For dessert I served my Pear and Raspberry Gateau. How well we eat when aboard *Daisy*.

[Cook's note]

Mum taught me to make this dish. It really produces the most tender, mouth-watering salmon. Baking in the airtight packets steams the salmon, trapping all the natural juices and the marinade and retaining all of the flavor. I rarely cook salmon any other way. I promise you if you try this, you will do it again and again. It's so simple and leaves you with very few dishes to clean up. This is good served over Coconut Rice with Mango—the flavors really complement one another.

Thai Spiced Salmon

1-inch piece fresh ginger, peeled and grated
1 teaspoon coriander seeds, crushed
½ teaspoon chili powder
1 tablespoon lime juice
½ teaspoon lime zest
1 teaspoon sesame oil
1 teaspoon lite soy sauce
4 salmon fillets, about 5 to 6 ounces each, with skin on
Cilantro leaves, for garnish

1. Preheat the oven to 375 degrees F.
2. In a small bowl, mix the ginger, coriander, chili powder, lime juice, lime zest, sesame oil, and soy sauce. Pour the mixture into a sealable plastic bag.
3. Place the salmon fillets in the bag and refrigerate for 30 minutes.
4. Tear off four large pieces of aluminum foil, approximately 1-foot square. Place one salmon fillet in the center of each foil square; top with a little of the marinade. Carefully fold the foil around the salmon to seal and make an airproof packet. Repeat for each salmon fillet.
5. Place the packets on a baking tray and bake in the center of the oven for 20 minutes.
6. Carefully remove the salmon from the foil: the steam in the packets could burn you.
    Garnish with cilantro. Serve at once.
    Enjoy.

[Cook's note]

This is one of those dishes that my children would possibly fly across the country for. Everyone who tries it absolutely loves it. Shredding the collard greens takes awhile, and if you don't have a deep fryer the fat splashing about can make a bit of a mess, but it's worth it. And it goes well served with just about anything.

Crispy Seaweed

1 bunch whole collard greens, approximately 10 large leaves
4 cups peanut oil, for frying
2 tablespoons fine sugar
1 teaspoon fine sea salt
1 tablespoon sesame seeds, toasted
1 level teaspoon ground cinnamon

1. Remove the white stems from the collard greens. Stack the leaves and roll them tightly into a cigar-like shape. Using a sharp knife, slice the collards into very thin shreds.
2. In a medium skillet, heat the peanut oil until almost smoking. To the oil add the shredded collards in small batches. (Be careful not to add too many of the collard greens at one time or the hot oil will splatter). Cook and stir for about 45 to 50 seconds. With a slotted spoon, gently remove the collards and drain on kitchen paper towels. Repeat this step until all the collards are cooked. Allow the oil to come back up to the correct heat in between each batch.
3. In a small bowl, mix the sugar, salt, sesame seeds, and cinnamon.
4. Place the cooked collards in batches into a large bowl. Sprinkle each batch with some of the sugar mix, lightly coating all of the collards.
5. The cooked collards will be extremely brittle, so handle as little as possible or you will end up with powdered collard greens.

The crispy seaweed will keep for several hours. Serve at room temperature. Enjoy.

[Cook's note]

My special friend Frieda made this dish while I was staying with her in Geneva. I couldn't believe how quickly she put it together, how beautiful it was to look at, and how mouthwateringly delicious it was to eat. Frieda made it with pears, but I have added raspberries here, as I love the combination of flavors.

Pear and Raspberry Gateau

1 large tin (14-ounce can) pear halves
¼ cup granulated sugar
2 cups fresh raspberries
1 sheet puff pastry
1 egg white, lightly beaten

1. Preheat the oven to 400 degrees F.
2. Drain the pears and set them aside on kitchen paper towels for a few minutes to absorb the extra juice.
3. Heat the sugar in a dry nonstick pan over high heat until it caramelizes (becomes liquid and turns brown but does not burn). Immediately pour the sugar into an ovenproof flan dish and tip the dish to completely cover the base with the caramel. (Note: The sugar will set very quickly, so be extremely careful when pouring the hot sugar.)
4. Slice each pear half into approximately 4 to 5 slices. Place the pear slices on top of the sugar, laying the pieces side by side, completely covering the base. Place the raspberries in the center and around the perimeter of the dish.
5. Roll out the puff pastry and place it on top of the pears, shaping to cover the entire dish. Tuck the excess pastry down around the edges between the pears and the edge of the flan dish. Brush the pastry with the egg white.
6. Place the flan dish on the center rack of the oven and bake for about 25 minutes.
7. Remove the flan dish from the oven. Place a serving plate over the top of the dish. Carefully flip it over so the pastry becomes the base and the caramelized pears and raspberries are on top. (Note: Use extreme caution when flipping the dish: the sugar will be liquid and scalding hot.)

Serve either at room temperature or cold from the fridge with a dollop of whipped cream.

Enjoy.

Chapter 4

Nevis to Montserrat

Coordinates: Montserrat 16 45'N 62 12'W

Tuesday, June 10

The crossing from Nevis to Montserrat took just five hours. We managed a respectable speed of 9 knots, with 15 to 18 knots of easterly wind. At half past twelve, we dropped anchor in Little Bay.

I'm so happy when Edi is on board with us because he always does anchor duty. I tend to be a bit of a liability when it comes to dropping the anchor, which requires a definite skill I've yet to acquire. Dropping the anchor without dropping the entire bloody thing really is quite important. I've done it, several times. Yes, the anchor, all 360 feet of chain, along with the tie-on thing at the end of the chain (called the bitter end) that's supposed to be idiot proof. The bitter end catches the end of the chain, securing it to the boat before it's lost on the seabed forever.

In the early afternoon we took *Whoops-a-Daisy* ashore to check in at the customs office. There we met a South African couple off a catamaran that we seemed to have followed for days. They also were making their way down the island chain to Grenada. I couldn't help noticing the woman's legs—they were perfect: long and slim, with a golden brown tan and not a mosquito bite in sight. I glanced down at my own shins and ankles and wondered why her legs weren't covered in itchy, swollen bites and scabs like mine. Did she have a secret mosquito repellent recipe? And how could I ask her without making it obvious that I had been looking at her legs? Just as I got up the courage to ask, they smiled and waved good-bye—and another mosquito bit me.

Once we had cleared customs, we set off for an island tour with George, a local taxi driver. We headed out through the villages of Davy Hill, Brades, and Cudjoe Head toward Salem in the south. Turning inland, George's taxi made its way along the rough- hewn roads that wiggle, twist, rise, dip and tilt all the way up to the Montserrat Volcano Observatory (MVO).

Soufriere Hills, Volcano, Montserrat.

During our drive, we stopped at the roadside to take photographs and pick mangos, filling an entire grocery bag with them. We couldn't resist eating a few. How can I begin to describe the heavenly taste of a mango that's picked fresh from the tree and warmed by the sun? The florescent yellow fruits were so abundant, they weighed down the tree branches and littered the roads. The air was heavy with the scent of mango.

We drove on through Brades, which after the 1995 Soufrière Hills volcanic eruption has emerged as the island hub. George pointed out where a new capitol is being constructed. Almost all of the island's major attractions were destroyed in the eruption. In fact, throughout Montserrat there's evidence of dislocation and deprivation alongside positive change and development. Despite suffering the enormous catastrophe, the people remain upbeat, warm, friendly, and happily optimistic.

We arrived at the MVO in time for the afternoon video showing, a vivid reminder of the incredibly destructive power of Mother Nature. The video showed Plymouth, the previous capital that had once been a beautiful little Caribbean town, pastel pretty with its colorful gingerbread houses and unique architecture. Today it all lies in ruins under a deep sea of thick gray ash.

As we left the observatory, we took photos of the smoking volcano, which appeared to us now as much too close for comfort. As we continued our drive around the island, George stopped next to a small fountain at the side of the road called Runaway Ghaut. Island legend says the water that flows from the mountain stream is some of the best in the Caribbean, and those who drink from the fountain will revisit Montserrat again and again. Edi and I took a drink, but Bob, who is always wary of his delicate stomach, couldn't be persuaded.

We continued on to the southern end of the island, which is still under constant threat from the volcano and even today remains an exclusion zone. (An exclusion zone is established by a sanctioning body, in this case the Montserrat government, to prohibit entry into a specific geographic area). George explained that the volcano was currently at low activity, and because no rain was forecast, we were allowed to enter the zone. Apparently rain causes huge slimy rivers of ash, creating treacherous driving conditions.

We drove quietly through one of the low-lying areas devastated by the eruption. George stopped the car so we could walk through the ruins of what had once been a beautiful golf course. Seeing the devastation up close, it was difficult to comprehend the reality of the tragedy. The rooftops of houses poked up through the ash. Wherever we looked there were stumps of dead trees and boulders the size of houses. It was a totally dead zone. It felt as though I were standing on the surface of the moon. The only activity came from the occasional clouds of rising ash, disturbed by little gusts of wind. Edi and I climbed through the second-story window of a house that had been buried in the ash. Dust-covered books still stood on the shelves. Broken pieces of furniture lay scattered around. The remnants were an eerie reminder of a previous life. We attempted to shake the ash from our shoes and clothes, got back into the car, and continued our drive.

Once back in the car, we continued up to Garibaldi Hill where we were promised a bird's-eye view of the town of Plymouth, the lush green mountains of the central hills, and the Caribbean Sea, with views across to Redonda and Nevis.

The drive up the hill was an adventure in itself. The road was not so much a road, more the remnants of a road. George's little car tipped and struggled over boulders and craters in the side of the hill, slipping and skidding as it made its way precariously on up. Then, as if the nerve-wracking climb up the steep hill wasn't enough excitement, we suddenly came across a humongous sleeping bull, sporting the largest pair of horns I've ever seen. It was right there in the middle of our path. George carefully maneuvered the car past the sleeping giant, and my eyes almost popped straight out of my head when I glimpsed the sheer drop beneath us. I immediately turned my gaze away from the possible death drop to look back to the enormous sleeping giant, which we were crawling unsteadily past, only to notice a lazy eyelid on the sleeping beast lift slowly, and an angry glare lock eyes with mine. This wouldn't have been difficult as I'm sure my eyes were as large as saucers.

I was more than a little nervous. If the beast had stood up, he could have quite easily pushed us over the edge. Edi and Bob appeared unconcerned. Maybe it's a guy thing, you know, "never show fear" or something like that. Whatever—I could care less about showing no fear: I was absolutely terrified. Bob and Edi actually appeared to be enjoying the drive up the hill. As we climbed higher, we could clearly see the trails left by the rivers of ash that had flowed from the top of the volcano down to the ocean below. One can only imagine the horror.

When the first eruption occurred there in the August of 1995, the formerly beautiful, defenseless little town of Plymouth was plunged into total darkness for fifteen minutes, as the thick cloud of rising ash hovered threateningly above it. Standing there on top of the hill looking down on the remnants of town beneath us, I could not even begin to imagine the terror suffered by those poor people. It was a sight I would not easily forget.

George gave us time to look around and take photos before returning to the car and starting our descent. I wasn't exactly thrilled at the prospect of the drive down the side of the hill: the drive up had aged me ten years.

As I predicted, the drive down proved to be a real heart stopper for me, as George took off at full speed. Bob caught sight of my terrified expression in the rearview mirror and asked George if he would mind slowing down so we could take some photos. It was really just a ploy to prevent the coronary that was threatening to occur right there behind him in the backseat.

Visions of our little car bouncing off a boulder and taking flight over the cliff edge, with all of us inside screaming like banshees as we plunged to our deaths in the thick sea of ash below, were all too vivid in my mind. We would all be engulfed in an ashy grave, and no one would ever find us. The words "last seen" established themselves firmly in my thoughts. I think I may have actually bruised Edi's arm with my viselike grip. After ten of the longest minutes in my life, we arrived safely at the foot of the hill, and I was able to breathe easily again. As I offered up a quick prayer of thanks, I realized that miracles do happen.

What I needed next was comfort food. I couldn't wait to return to my cozy galley to prepare that night's dinner: Daisy's Nutty Caribbean Curried Chicken Salad followed by English Treacle Tart.

Wednesday, June 11

After what can only be described as another memorable day, we were blessed once again with a beautiful sunny morning. We took the dinghy ashore to explore Rendezvous Bay, the only white sand beach on Montserrat. It's only accessible from the ocean by boat or on foot along a precarious trail over a steep bluff that's definitely not for the weak or fainthearted. Consequently, the only crowds on this lovely little beach are the hermit crabs and the gulls.

There's a derelict house on the beach, and I couldn't help but wonder not only why someone would build in such a remote and difficult location but also how they managed to build there, with accessibility being so difficult. There were no visible roads or paths and no dock. No wonder it was abandoned. I couldn't imagine anyone living there for long.

We attempted to snorkel, but the sea was rough and the current very strong. Several times we had to rescue *Whoops-a-Daisy* from being washed out to sea. We couldn't get the little dinghy anchor to set. There was nowhere to tie it up on the beach, so we finally gave up and went back to *Daisy* to set sail for Guadeloupe.

[Cook's note]

I first ate something resembling this dish at a buffet about thirty years ago. The flavors were so amazing, I had to rush home and write them down. It took awhile to get it just right, but it's pretty foolproof now. Everyone who tries it absolutely loves it. If you make it a day ahead, the chicken (or tofu) has a chance to really absorb the curry flavors, making it even tastier. I love dishes like this: quick, easy, and delicious. Admittedly, the ingredients look a little odd. People watching me make this dish always raise their eyebrows when they see what goes into it, but I promise the ingredients work and the taste is amazing.

For a vegetarian option, replace the chicken with 8 ounces of firm tofu, drained and diced into half-inch cubes.

Daisy's Nutty Caribbean Curried Chicken Salad

1 teaspoon olive oil
1 red onion, peeled and medium diced
3 scallions, white and green parts, roughly chopped
1 medium celery stalk, chopped
3 tablespoons tomato ketchup
4 tablespoons apricot preserves
2 teaspoons hot curry powder
3 cloves garlic, peeled and roughly chopped
Juice of 1 lemon
1 3- to 4-pound rotisserie chicken
1½ cups mayonnaise
¼ cup dried apricots, finely chopped
½ cup cashew nuts, roughly chopped
Salt and freshly ground pepper

1. Heat the oil in a medium-size saucepan over medium heat. Add the onion and fry, stirring frequently until soft but not brown. Pour off the oil and add the scallions, celery, tomato ketchup, apricot preserves, curry powder, garlic, and lemon juice. Cook for another 5 minutes, stirring frequently. Remove from the heat and allow to cool for about 30 minutes.

2. Dice the cooked chicken and set it aside.
3. Once the onion mixture cools, puree the mix with an immersion blender to a smooth paste. (If you don't have an immersion blender, use a liquidizer or mortar and pestle to blend the mix.)
4. In a large bowl, add the mayonnaise to the pureed mix, stirring well to combine. Add the apricots, cashew nuts, and salt and pepper to taste. Mix the diced chicken into the cooled mixture, cover the bowl with plastic wrap, and refrigerate for 2 hours, or preferably overnight.

I like to serve this with a small green salad and a baked potato.

Enjoy.

[Cook's note]

Really going back to my roots here, this was another of my nan's favorite things to bake (but only in the winter months because in the heat of the summer the syrup would attract flies from miles away).

English Treacle Tart (also known as Shoo Fly Pie)

1½ cups (approximately) golden syrup (available in the international aisle of most supermarkets, in the English section)
¾ cup fresh white breadcrumbs
½ cup almonds, ground
1 large free-range egg
¾ cup heavy cream
Shortcrust pastry*, chilled (or 1 8-inch unbaked deep-dish pie shell)

One day ahead: Put all the ingredients (except the pastry) into a blender and blend until smooth. Place the mixture in a covered container and refrigerate overnight.

1. Preheat the oven to 350 degrees F.
2. Roll out the chilled pastry to form an 8-inch round. Press the round pastry to line an 8-inch shallow pie plate. Cut a sheet of baking parchment paper to fit inside the pastry. Cover the parchment paper with baking beans or uncooked rice; fill to the top of the pie plate. *(Note: Baking beans are ceramic or clay beads that weigh the pastry down during the initial baking, before the pie contents are added. They allow the pastry to precook but prevent it from rising. If baking beans are not available, uncooked rice can be used as a substitute.)*
3. Bake the pastry for 15 minutes. Remove the baking beans (or rice) and allow the pastry case to cool for about 20 minutes.
4. Pour the chilled filling evenly into the pastry case and bake for 15 minutes. Lower the heat to 300 degrees F (gas mark 2) and bake for another 35 minutes.
5. Remove the tart from the oven and allow it to cool for 15 to 30 minutes. Serve cold with a dollop of whipped cream.
   Enjoy.

*Shortcrust pastry is a half-fat-to-flour-ratio pastry.

Parmesan Eggs Baked in Tomatoes

4 medium tomatoes, ripe but firm
1 clove garlic, chopped
4 extra-large free-range eggs
Salt and freshly ground black pepper
1 tablespoon tomato puree
2 tablespoons heavy cream
1 teaspoon fresh marjoram, chopped (or ½ teaspoon dried marjoram)
4 heaping teaspoons grated Parmesan
4 slices bread of your choice
2 tablespoons unsalted butter
2 teaspoons olive oil
½ cup fresh basil leaves, shredded

1. Preheat the oven to 350 degrees F.
2. Wash the tomatoes, wipe them dry, and slice off the tops. Carefully spoon out the pulp and sprinkle the inside of the shells with salt. Turn the tomato shells upside down on kitchen paper towels to drain for about 30 minutes.
3. Turn the tomatoes over and sprinkle the garlic inside the shells. Carefully break one egg into each tomato shell. Season with a little salt and freshly ground pepper.
4. In a small bowl, blend the tomato puree, cream, and marjoram; spoon the mixture gently over the eggs. Sprinkle 1 teaspoon Parmesan over each tomato.
5. Place the tomatoes in an ovenproof dish; bake near the top of the oven for 20 to 25 minutes, or until the eggs have just set.
6. Meanwhile, with a 2-inch cutter cut the bread slices into rounds. Heat the butter and oil in a pan over medium heat until hot but not smoking, and fry the bread until crisp and golden on both sides.
7. When the eggs are set, arrange one tomato on each round of bread, sprinkle the shredded basil over the tops, and serve at once.
   Enjoy.

Chapter 5
Montserrat to Guadeloupe

Coordinates: Guadeloupe 16 15'N 61 35'W

We weighed anchor at midday and enjoyed the sail across, with a gentle, steady wind averaging 12 to 18 knots. We once again managed a respectably consistent 9 knots, arriving in Guadeloupe at 6 p.m. It was too late to clear customs, so we stayed on board for the evening, dropping anchor in Deshaies Bay. The South African couple we had seen in the Montserrat customs office was there once again in the bay just ahead of us. That night for our dinner I made my Sweet Crust Fish Pie, followed by Daisy's Yogurt Berry Surprise.

Thursday, June 12

We were up early to have breakfast and go ashore to clear customs. The office was only a short walk from the dock but up a very steep hill. It was only nine in the morning, but the temperature was already rising fast. I was sure I could feel the soles of my flip-flops melting on the red-hot sidewalk. Panting and soaked with perspiration, we arrived at the office, only to discover a Closed sign on the door. We stood there with slumped shoulders wondering what to do next, when I noticed that the office door was slightly ajar. I could see someone inside, so I cautiously pushed the door open. Luckily for us, a pleasant customs officer invited us in. And despite the fact that the office was officially closed, she agreed to clear us in. Quite possibly the sight of my sweaty purple face and heavy breathing may have persuaded her not to send us back out into the heat, where she may have been faced with the prospect of calling out the paramedics.

After customs, we walked the short distance into town. We found a little boulangerie, where we enjoyed a breakfast of really delicious coffee and croissants. Sitting there at the side of the road, I felt as though we easily could have been at a seaside village cafe in the South of France.

We walked around the small town, taking photographs and window-shopping. I bought some postcards and Bob rented a car. We stopped in a charming deli and bought some mini pizzas, delicious pastries, and icy cold bottles of Pellegrino before heading out of town and following the coast road.

Guadeloupe, which is part of France, was originally known as Karukera ("Island of Pretty Waters"). It has a population of around 400,000 and is actually composed of two islands Basse-Terre and Grande-Terre they form the shape of a lopsided butterfly. The Rivière Salée separates the two islands, and Basse-Terre is the larger of the two. We drove out through Pointe Ferry, where we stopped on the coast to eat lunch, and then continued on through Baille-Argent and Pointe-Noire.

At Anse Guyonneau we headed inland to the interior. We drove up the mountain road into the rain forest, where we stopped near a beautiful waterfall. Two nuns were knelt deep in prayer at an altar that was built into the rock beside the waterfall. After prayer, they washed their faces in the crystal clear water from the falls before quietly moving on. The three of us wandered around taking photographs and admiring the amazing scenery. We explored the area before heading back to the car and continuing our climb on up to the Monastery St. Joseph. The views from the top overlooking the rain forest beneath us were quite breathtaking.

From the Monastery St. Joseph, we drove on to the botanical gardens situated within the rain forest. Here beautiful open areas within the grounds housed raccoons, monkeys, parrots, tortoises, otters, and many other wild creatures.

Edi and I stopped to watch an old, blind, extremely overweight raccoon eat his lunch. He sat in the shade of the surrounding trees, reaching around with his paws to locate the food that he was sitting in the middle of. He was obviously savoring every mouthful. Once he was convinced that all the food was gone, he toppled over onto his back with his legs in the air and fell asleep. Edi and I laughed so much it brought tears to our eyes.

Sixty feet above the gardens, precarious looking narrow bridges formed a walkway, just two planks wide, strung through the treetops. Without really giving it too much thought, I followed along behind Bob and Edi, and before I knew what was happening, I was being fitted into a full body harness. This proved to be an awkward and uncomfortable procedure, as I happened to be wearing a dress.

The young man who was struggling to fit me into my harness directed me to remove my shoes. Within minutes, we were all appropriately harnessed, instructed on safety procedures, and ready to go. We climbed cautiously up the ladder to the first platform. I nervously stayed close behind Edi, feeling more than a little self-conscious in my daft-looking outfit. I followed Edi's lead and carefully hooked my safety lines on before starting the climb out along the swinging bridges. Feeling my way cautiously along the wooden planks and trying not to think too much about the sixty-foot drop beneath me, I moved sloth-like across the swinging walkways. With my eyes squeezed shut, I proceeded farther across the swinging death trap. Previous concerns about my appearance were quickly forgotten as the bridge's wooden planks creaked and swayed under our weight. White-knuckled, I made my way precariously and slowly behind Edi. I couldn't help but wonder how on earth I had allowed myself to do this.

As frightened as I was, once I actually opened my eyes I found viewing the beauty of the forest from the treetops an exhilarating experience. I kept silently reminding myself that my safety harness was securely attaching me to the safety lines. The farther we went along, the higher the walkways climbed. Miraculously, by the time we came to the end, we were all a little less nervous. I just wished I'd been allowed to carry my camera. No one would believe I did this without some sort of photographic evidence. I'm glad I accomplished this aerial walk and would do it again (dressed more suitably for the occasion next time).

In the late afternoon we left the gardens and drove back down the winding roads, which were surprisingly some of the most well-maintained roads I've driven on in a long time. As we continued toward the capital of Pointe-à-Pitre, I sensed we had taken a wrong turn when our deserted, dusty two-lane road suddenly became a four-lane highway, jammed in both directions with French cars. The highway was lined with high-rise apartment buildings, large supermarkets, stores, industrial sites, and business offices.

The streets were bustling with people hurrying along in all directions: Business people in suits carrying briefcases, women with children in tow carrying shopping bags with baguettes poking out. Sidewalk cafes with people reading newspapers, sipping coffee, and smoking Gauloises. The atmosphere and appearance was typical of any French town. Suddenly, this didn't feel like a Caribbean Island—at least not the Caribbean I'd become accustomed to.

Guadeloupe is financially supported by Paris and provides a much higher standard of living than most of the other Caribbean countries. Guadeloupe's main export used to be sugarcane, but that's been replaced by bananas, which account for about fifty percent of export earnings. Sugarcane is still widely grown here and used mainly for making rum. The sugar accounts for about forty percent of agricultural land, although today tourism is rapidly becoming the island's biggest earner.

We continued out through the center of town toward the marina, where we parked the car and walked around to sightsee. We did some shopping and stopped for a beer at one of the local bars on the harbor front in Point-à-Pitre.

Rush hour was in full swing as we made our way back to Deshaies. We ended up sitting in heavy traffic as we found ourselves in a convoy of the local population making their way home. We drove out through colorful villages, full of little villas and houses all painted in delicate pastel shades. We saw brightly painted roadside stalls selling locally grown produce like mangos, tomatoes, papayas, bananas, potatoes, breadfruit, and much more.

We arrived back at Deshaies in the early evening and stopped for dinner at a fabulous seafront restaurant, Movillages, which was really lovely. Our table looked out over the bay, so we watched the beautiful sunset as we dined. It was a fitting end to a very enjoyable day.

Friday, June 13

In the morning Bob and I took *Whoops-a-Daisy* ashore to visit the Internet cafe. Bob needed to send a fax, and we both wanted to use the Internet. As it turned out, the fax wouldn't send and (not surprisingly) there was no Internet. This is not unusual for the Caribbean islands. The trip wasn't a complete waste of time: we found the post office and I was able to send my postcards. As I handed them over to the post office assistant, I couldn't help thinking that it was very possible that I would be back home months before the postcards arrived. The Caribbean is not known for its speedy postal service. Before returning to *Daisy*, I did a little provisioning at the local supermarket. Meanwhile, Bob returned the car to the rental agency. Having completed as many jobs as possible, we took the groceries back to the boat in readiness for the next leg of our trip.

Relaxing with a cold beer

Before noon we weighed anchor and set sail for Iles des Saintes. I served a very quick lunch while underway. The storm clouds were gathering and the skies were growing darker by the minute. Bob hadn't wanted to waste any time with our departure. The wind was building in strength, and we suddenly found ourselves having to deal with 40-knot winds, heavy rain, thunder, and lightning.

The violence of the sea scares the living daylights out of me. My active imagination kicks in at the slightest sign of trouble. And as the storm picked up, every impulse in my being was screaming at me, "Run for your life!" My fear of disaster at sea came flooding back, and I'm ashamed to say that I left Edi and Bob to deal with it. Like a rabbit scampering to its burrow, I bolted to the safety of my cabin below. I dived under the comforter on my bed where I stayed put, trying desperately to smother my bloody imagination that was running riot in my head like a hamster on crack. I'm not a great sailor—in fact, I'm not even a mediocre sailor—and I'm absolutely terrified of storms at sea. It's something I'll never get used to.

We eventually arrived at Terre-de-Haut and dropped anchor in the bay; I was a little shaken and feeling slightly nauseated, but thankfully all in one piece.

The rain poured throughout the day as the skies grew darker and darker. We all stayed on board, safe in the confines of our floating refuge. Bob, by some small stroke of luck, was able to pick up an Internet signal and work all afternoon. Edi watched *West Wing* on TV, and I kept myself busy in the galley baking—a pastime that always relaxes me. Preparing food is one of my favorite things to do and has always been a great distraction for me in times of stress.

[Cook's note]

Following many disastrous attempts to make a delicious fish pie, I finally hit a home run with this one. The biscuit topping is a real success; it adds a sweet taste and a dumpling-like texture, contrasting well with the creamy sauce, flaky fish, and vegetables. I use cod for this recipe, but any firm white fish, such as sea bass or halibut, could be substituted.

Sweet Crust Fish Pie

1¾ pound cod fillets, cut into 2-inch squares
Salt and pepper
5 tablespoons unsalted butter, divided
1 tablespoon fresh tarragon leaves, stems removed
1 large leek (both white and green parts), chopped into ½-inch slices
4 ounces (8 tablespoons) frozen peas
4 medium carrots, peeled and chopped into ½-inch slices
1 tablespoon all-purpose flour
4 tablespoons whole milk
¼ cup heavy cream
1 tablespoon dill, finely chopped
1 can buttermilk biscuits (such as refrigerated Pillsbury biscuits)
Spray olive oil

1. Preheat the oven to 375 degrees F.
2. Season the cod with salt and pepper. Melt 1 tablespoon butter in a large sauté pan over medium heat. Cook the cod pieces on both sides until lightly golden in color, about 2 to 3 minutes per side. Remove the cod from the pan and place it in a large ovenproof flan dish. Sprinkle the tarragon leaves over the fish.
3. Add about 1 teaspoon butter and the chopped leeks to the sauté pan; cook for about 5 to 6 minutes, until just starting to soften. Add the frozen peas and stir for 1 minute. Remove the leeks and peas from the pan and spread them over the cod.
4. Place the chopped carrots in salted, rapidly boiling water for 3 to 4 minutes. Drain the carrots and spread them evenly over the cod.

To make the roux:

1. Heat the rest of the butter (approximately 3½ tablespoons) in a saucepan over medium heat until it is reduced to liquid. Remove the pan from the heat; with a wooden spoon, gradually stir in the flour until all the flour is incorporated. Gradually add the milk, stirring constantly to achieve a smooth, thick paste.

2. Return the pan to the medium heat and slowly add the cream. Continue stirring until all the cream is incorporated. Add the dill and continue to cook gently over the lowest heat setting, without boiling, for about 10 minutes.

3. Pour the roux evenly over the cod and vegetables.

4. Open the biscuits and carefully pull each one apart into two halves. Cover the cod and vegetables with the biscuit halves. Lightly spray the biscuits with olive oil.

5. Bake for 35 to 40 minutes or until the biscuits are golden brown. Enjoy.

[Cook's note]

This wickedly decadent dish is one of my family's absolute favorites—but it's not a low-calorie dish, so we keep it for special occasions. The crunchy sugar top covering a slightly tart, creamy yogurt mix is a delightful contrast to the sweet berries buried beneath, hence the "surprise"!

Daisy's Yogurt Berry Surprise

1½ cups fresh berries (anything in season) plus extra for garnish
¼ cup amaretto liqueur
½ cup mascarpone cheese
1 tablespoon raspberry jam
1 cup whipping cream
1 cup natural (or plain) yogurt
1 tablespoon demerara or dark brown sugar

1. Clean the berries. (If using strawberries, slice them in half.) Spread the berries evenly over the bottom of an 8-inch glass flan dish. Add the amaretto, stirring gently to coat all the berries.
2. In a small bowl, gently stir the mascarpone with the raspberry jam to combine; spoon it over the berries.
3. In a medium bowl, with an electric hand mixer beat the whipping cream until stiff peaks form. Gently stir in the natural yogurt, mixing well.
4. Spread the cream mixture over the mascarpone and berries; sprinkle liberally with the dark brown sugar. Refrigerate for at least two hours before serving.
   Garnish with berries.
   Enjoy.

Chapter 6
Iles des Saintes to Dominica

Coordinates: Iles des Saintes 15 18'N 61 23W

Saturday, June 14

We woke around 6:30 a.m. and were relieved to find that the storm had passed. In its wake came brilliant sunshine that streamed through the hatches. I made scrambled eggs with smoked salmon, freshly squeezed orange juice, and some delicious coffee and cinnamon rolls for breakfast. Then Bob, Edi, and I all went ashore to try and locate the local Internet cafe.

I e-mailed Mum, Niki, and Danni to let them know all was well and we were still alive. After a bad crossing, I'm always keen to let everyone know we're OK; it never occurs to me that anyone would even be aware of the sort of crossing we would have had.

Once we finished with the Internet, Edi and I explored the town of Bourg, the only town on the island of Terre-de-Haut, which is just 3 miles long and 2 miles wide. We window-shopped while Bob stayed at the cafe on his computer, trying to reserve flights back to the United States for work later in the month.

We bought ice cream and sat on a bench at the side of the road, fighting a losing battle trying to eat the ice cream faster than it was melting. Edi and I couldn't resist the local stores; he enjoys shopping as much as I do. I bought him a really cool ring, made locally from stainless steel. I also found some pretty starfish earrings for myself. I quickly resisted the temptation to buy them, however, once I caught sight of the $1,800 price tag.

Back on board, I served a quick lunch before we weighed anchor to head off to Dominica, our next port of call. We had a great sail over, so much more pleasant than our previous leg. About 4 miles off shore, we spotted a humpback whale. The whale was just lying there sleeping on top of the water, basking in the sunshine and blowing water from its blowhole. We watched it for about five minutes before deciding to see if we could get closer. We brought the sails in because the wind had dropped to a pathetic 5 knots and turned in the direction of the whale. Although we approached slowly and cautiously, *Daisy*'s engine must have woken it because all of a sudden the enormous flippers waved at us. The whale rolled and splashed in the waves before performing a spectacular leap out of the water and disappearing into the inky depths below. What an incredible sight! I've seen this on television many times, but that doesn't compare to seeing a whale up close and personal. A few minutes later we spotted two waterspouts behind us. Once again Bob slowed the engine, and we watched patiently as the waterspouts appeared to come in our direction. We waited, hoping to get another glimpse of these magnificent creatures. Unfortunately, it wasn't to be: after a few minutes, the whales turned and headed back out to sea. It was getting late, so we cranked up the engines and headed for shore.

A Humpback whale swimming alongside Daisy

One of the many joys of sailing is sharing the warm waters of the Caribbean with the humpback whales, who visit during the winter months to breed and calve. The whales have to live off their fat reserves, or blubber, because there is much less food for them in the warm, clear Caribbean waters. The reason the water in the Caribbean is so clear is because it's not as productive as the northern waters; there are fewer phytoplankton, zooplankton, and fish for the whales to feed upon. This is the reason the northern seas are so murky and the southern seas clear. While there's a greater diversity of life, tropical waters don't contain the immense schools of fish and plankton found farther north. In northern waters, an adult humpback whale can eat up to a ton of food a day. The males can grow up to fifty-seven feet in length, but the females can grow up to an amazing sixty-two feet long and weigh as much as fifty tons.

The humpback is the most popular whale on whale-watching trips and often appears happy to put on a performance. They are very acrobatic, breaching high out of the water and slapping the waves as they come back down. The humpback has also been seen spy hopping: poking its head up out of the water, looking around for a few seconds, then submerging again. The humpback will also display lob tailing: waving its tail in the air and slapping the water loudly. They will often

approach boats, showing little evidence of shyness toward humans. They don't usually pose a threat to boats, and there's no reason to fear them if they approach. Some whale watchers turn their engines off to hear the humpback's eerie songs through the hull.

In 1988, Dominica was the first of the eastern Caribbean islands to offer whale-watching tours. Besides the humpback, sperm, pilot, false killer, and pygmy sperm whales as well as spotted, spinner, bottlenose, Risso's, and Fraser dolphins frequent these friendly waters.

As we approached the island of Dominica, we were in total awe. This was the most beautiful island we had seen so far. Each island had seemed more beautiful than the last, but Dominica was definitely the prettiest. It was mountainous, lush, and so very green. The rain forests looked incredible, and I couldn't wait to go ashore and explore.

As we headed toward the anchorage, a little motorboat came out to greet us. The guy at the helm introduced himself as Martin and then guided us to a safe spot to anchor. We were in Coconut Bay, Portsmouth. Once we were safely anchored, Martin, a local tour guide, told us about his island sightseeing trips. We arranged to take the river tour at 7 a.m. the next the morning.

I prepared another delicious dinner of Crispy Coconut Shrimp followed by Crème Brûlée. We all agreed that this had been an amazing trip so far, and we were very excited about the next day's island tour.

Sunday, June 15

Martin arrived promptly at 7 a.m. and transported us in his little motorboat to the shore, where he left us while he collected seven more people who were to join us on the tour. We all climbed into Martin's wooden rowboat (outboards are not allowed on the Indian River) and set off up the beautiful river.

As Martin rowed, he explained some island history. He told us of Dominica's eight dormant volcanoes that have provided the island with very rich soil. Just about anything will grow here. Dominica exports fruit and vegetables to most of the other islands. Bananas make up the main crop, but there are also sugarcane, limes, avocados, mangos, ginger, vanilla, watercress, yams, sweet potatoes, pineapples, coffee beans, and coconuts—and much more than I can list here.

Dominica is the largest of the Windward Islands with a population of about 72,000. Unlike on the other islands, there are no casinos or multinational chain resorts—at least not yet. From what I could tell, the island appeared to be totally unspoiled. The island's main attraction is its raw natural beauty with fabulous waterfalls, rain forest pools and rivers, forest hiking trails, and spectacular diving sites.

As we made our way slowly up the river, Martin explained that there are 365 rivers in Dominica, and the Indian River was named after the original island inhabitants, the Carib Indians. He pointed out the hundreds of land crabs on the riverbanks. The red crabs, with their bright red backs and white claws, could easily be mistaken for fallen flowers. Hundreds of gray mullet swarmed in schools around our boat, and we even spotted an occasional barracuda. The wild hibiscus flowers that had dropped into the river from the overhead branches floated like lilies on the surface of the water.

Hummingbirds hovered above us, feeding from the many flowers growing wild on the trees. Martin pointed out a hummingbird's nest. It wasn't much bigger than a golf ball. He told us that the chicks are so tiny when they hatch, they look like large flies.

Hummingbirds are extremely high-energy birds with a cruising speed of 25 mph and a diving speed of 85 mph. They need a constant supply of nectar to keep their energy levels flowing, and they pollinate other flowers as they feed. They're also extremely territorial and can often be spotted in fierce battles, defending their territory.

Martin pointed out the *Heliconia caribaea*, a magnificent flowering plant that collects water for hummingbirds to use as drinking troughs. He pulled the boat over to the riverbank and got out to show us his skill of skinning coconuts with a machete, something he had been doing since he was eleven years old. He handed a coconut to each man in the boat as a gift for Father's Day.

The river was picture perfect in its natural beauty, with the shafts of sunlight breaking through the overhead canopy and reflecting off the water. The only sounds came from the insects, the birds, and the gentle splash of Martin's oars as he rowed us farther upriver. We all sat in silence, mesmerized by the beauty around us. Martin pointed out a site where a scene from the *Pirates of the Caribbean 2* had been filmed. Before the filmmakers departed, they had considerately restored the area to its original condition.

We next stopped at one of the forest gardens, where everyone got out of the boat to view different banana trees and wildlife indigenous to Dominica. We saw lizards, herons, and more hummingbirds, along with many different plants and fruit trees. I took dozens of photographs. Martin peeled a pineapple and gave everyone a slice; it was incredible—warm from the sun and really sweet and juicy.

Time passed quickly, and before long we were heading back in the little boat. Once ashore, Martin was kind enough to drive Bob, Edi, and me to the customs office, where we were able to check in and out again. But unlike the river tour, the van ride was anything but peaceful: The roads on Dominica are without a doubt the worst roads I've experienced anywhere. They're full of potholes, huge ones, and drivers swerve violently all over the place like they're blind drunk in their vain attempts to avoid the craters. Other than the roads, the island is absolutely lovely and well worth a visit.

It's said that if Christopher Columbus were to return to the Caribbean to-day, the only island he would recognize would be Dominica. Having now visited the island, I can see why: it's so totally unspoiled.

We hurried back into Martin's motorboat, and he sped us back to *Daisy* so we could quickly get underway. We were under pressure to reach Martinique before dark, and Bob was very keen to get started. While Bob and Edi cast off, I prepared lunch. We had a really great sail across, completing the 65 miles in just eight hours. About 4 miles off shore we spotted a school of dolphins, jumping and playing not far from the boat. We slowed to watch them for a while.

We arrived in St. Pierre, Martinique, just before sunset, around 6 p.m. We dropped anchor in the bay, and because I was so tired, dinner was Welsh rarebit (cheese on toast) and beans, nothing gourmet from Daisy's galley that night.

Edi could never resist getting his feet wet!

Bob and Edi taking a dip.

Me shopping in Dominica.

Crispy Coconut Shrimp

1 fresh coconut, cracked and flesh removed
¾ cup Panko breadcrumbs
1 teaspoon ground star anise
2 egg whites
1 pound large raw shrimp, peeled and deveined, tail left on
(Note: Leaving the tail on makes dipping the shrimp in the egg white and breadcrumbs less messy, and it looks pretty.)
1 lemon, cut into wedges, for garnish

1. Preheat the oven to 375 degrees F.
2. Using a hand grater, grate the flesh of the coconut into course shreds.
3. In a small bowl, mix the coconut with the breadcrumbs and star anise; set aside.
4. In a separate small bowl, use a whisk to beat the egg whites until foamy but not stiff.
5. Dip each shrimp first into the egg white and then into the breadcrumbs and coconut mix. Repeat to form a double coating.
6. Place the shrimp on a sheet pan lined with baking parchment; bake on the top oven rack for 8 to 10 minutes.
    Serve with a lemon wedge and a fresh green salad.
    Enjoy.

[Cook's note]
This is my husband's all-time favorite dessert, and fortunately it's one of the easiest desserts to make. This mix will fill nine ramekins.

Crème Brûlée

2 extra-large free-range eggs
4 egg yolks (from extra-large free-range eggs)
½ cup sugar plus 9 heaping teaspoons for caramelizing
3 cups heavy cream
1 tablespoon Grand Marnier
1 teaspoon pure vanilla extract
The seeds scraped from 1 vanilla bean

1. Preheat the oven to 300 degrees F.
2. In a medium bowl, gently beat the eggs and sugar together; set aside.
3. In a medium-size heavy-based saucepan, scald the cream until hot but not boiling.
    Gradually add the cream to the eggs and stir gently.
4. To the cream and eggs add the Grand Marnier, vanilla, and vanilla bean seeds; stir gently. Pour the mix into ramekins.
5. Place the ramekins in a deep ovenproof pan; fill the pan halfway up the sides of the ramekins with boiling water.
6. Bake for 40 to 50 minutes. (Note: The crème brûlée should jiggle a little when removed from the oven. Don't worry: it will be cooked. And it will set in the refrigerator.)
7. Cool, then refrigerate for 2 hours before serving.
    To serve: Sprinkle about 1 heaping teaspoon of sugar on the top of the cold brûlée and caramelize with a blowtorch (or under a hot broiler) to achieve a hard golden-caramel topping.
    Enjoy.

Chapter 7

Martinique to St. Lucia

Coordinates: Martinique 14 40'N 61 00'W, St. Lucia 14 1'N 60 59'W

Monday, June 16

Sadly, with no time to explore Martinique, we left St. Pierre at 8:30 a.m. to sail straight down to St. Lucia. We were under pressure to arrive in St. Lucia by the end of the day to pick up Ed's friend Justin, who was coming aboard with us for a few weeks. And Bob was scheduled to make a conference call by 4 p.m.

Just a couple of miles off shore, we encountered a large school of spinner dolphins—maybe as many as 100. It was the largest group of dolphins I had seen so far. They were racing along with the boat, leaping and jumping all around us. I was trying to take photographs. Bob slowed down so we could get a better look, but the dolphins got bored and swam away. Then we increased the engine speed, and sure enough they all turned around and came back to swim and race with the boat again. They were playfully showing off: leaping out of the water, twisting and turning, performing acrobatic feats, and spinning in the air, which is how they came by their name. It was exhilarating to watch them race along in the wake of the boat and swim on either side of the bow. Bob and I laughed out loud when a large dolphin leaped high out the water by the stern of the boat and slapped the water playfully with its tail as it dived back in. They swam with and around the boat for a full fifteen minutes before moving on. We watched as they swam away and we continued on toward St. Lucia. Watching the dolphins in their natural environment and being so close to them will never cease to thrill me. What a wonderful start to our day.

Sailing down island from Martinique, the capital appeared like any other large city, just in a much prettier setting. As usual, I found the sail a little uncomfortable. So, not wishing to break with tradition, I slept for most of the leg. We arrived at Rodney Bay, St. Lucia, at 3 p.m. Rodney Bay is a port of entrance and a good place to clear in. Once we were safely anchored in the bay, Bob went ashore to make his 4 p.m. conference call. Meanwhile, Edi and I set about cleaning and organizing the boat, preparing for Justin, who arrived promptly at 7 p.m. We ate dinner on board: Barbecued Tofu and Pineapple-Vegetable Skewers followed by decadent Daisy's Chocolate Mousse. After dinner, Edi and Justin went ashore to a local bar, Bob worked on his computer, and I read in bed. Just another day in paradise!

Tuesday, June 17

Bob and I went ashore at 8 a.m. to use the Internet cafe. I reluctantly booked Edi's flight home, and Bob made another conference call. I picked up some provisions from the store; predictably for a harbor store, the selection was not great, or fresh, and the prices were high. We got back to the boat before noon, ate lunch, then weighed anchor, setting sail to move down island.

The famous 'hanging' rock from the movie 'Pirates of The Caribbean'

Bob, Edi and Justin on the old film set for 'Pirates of The Caribbean'.

Light bulb needs changing at the top of Daisy's mast, Justin, 86 feet up in the air.

We picked up a mooring in a beautiful bay right between the Pitons. Edi and Justin went snorkeling, while Bob and I prepared dinner. Bob grilled filet mignon on the barbecue, while I stir-fried some vegetables. Many boat vendors came up to *Daisy*, offering fresh fish, T-shirts, locally made jewelry, ornaments, and groceries. I ordered vegetables from one of them to be brought around in the morning. After dinner, we sat up on deck with a cocktail and enjoyed the magnificent sunset.

To our amazement, Edi discovered that we could pick up the Internet. Who would have thought, sitting there in a quiet little bay beneath the Pitons, that we would get an Internet signal? I sent e-mails to my mum and the girls, and Bob managed to get some more work done. There was a lovely cooling breeze in the bay that night, and we all got a great night's sleep.

Wednesday, June 18

We woke early to move the boat to the other end of the bay for Edi and Justin to snorkel again. The local vendor brought my vegetables and ice. A fruit called chayote was among the selection of locally grown produce he brought. It looked like a large, wrinkled, bright green pear. I later discovered that chayote is usually cooked, but it can be used raw in salsas or salads. The fruit is a good source of amino acids and vitamin C. The root, stem, seeds, and leaves of the plant are also edible. The tubers are prepared much like potatoes, while the shoots and leaves can be eaten in salads and stir-fries. It does not need to be peeled, and it can also be boiled, stuffed, baked, mashed, or fried. The flavor is rather bland and benefits from plenty of seasoning (such as in a curry or another well-spiced dish).

A pretty little pair of swifts spent some time checking out the boat as a nesting place; they were particularly interested in the hollow in *Daisy*'s boom. I watched them while I waited for the boys to return from snorkeling. Swifts are notorious for building their nests on boats and ships; one has to wonder, do they follow the ships when they set sail? There wasn't much chance of these two building their nest on *Daisy* because we were about to set sail. We were heading to St. Vincent and eating breakfast en route.

Once again we were lucky enough to see our friends the dolphins as well as a large marlin that jumped clear out of the water. Flying fish were everywhere, amazing us with their ability to soar above the water for incredible distances. The sail was quite rough as we proceeded, with winds gusting to over 30 knots. About an hour from shore, we had yet another visit from a school of dolphins. This time I identified them as striped dolphins. These beautiful animals appear almost hand-painted. With an upward brush stroke toward the dorsal fin, the light gray flank divides the dark back and the white or pink belly. The easiest identifying feature is a thin, dark stripe extending from the black beak around the eye patch to the underside of the rear flank. They were jumping and swimming with the bow of the boat, while we were all on the bow watching. I snapped as many photographs as I could, but there were so many dolphins all around *Daisy* I mostly got shots of tails and splashes. I don't think David Attenborough will be offering me a job with his film crew anytime soon.

We arrived at Young Island, off the tip of St. Vincent, at 6:45 p.m., just around sunset. Young Island is a thirty-five-acre privately owned island that truly fulfills what most people think of as the "Caribbean dream." It's virtually a tropical garden with all its lush green foliage, fruits, and flowering plants growing with splendid, manicured abundance all over the little island. Pretty palm-fringed sandy paths lead to luxurious thatched cottages. Garden hammocks swing gently between the tall palms, delicious cocktails are served in coconuts, and the beaches have powdery, soft white sand. This island resort is about as close to paradise as you will find in this part of the Caribbean. This time Young Island was only an overnight stop on our way to the Tobago Cays.

Barbecued Tofu and Pineapple-Vegetable Skewers

1 (8-ounce) package firm tofu, drained, dried, and cut into cubes
¾ cup brown sugar
3 tablespoons boiling water
1 tablespoon dark soy sauce
1 tablespoon oyster sauce
2 large cloves garlic, peeled and finely diced
1-inch piece fresh ginger, peeled and diced
2 tablespoons rice wine
1 teaspoon sesame oil
½ teaspoon Maldon sea salt flakes
½ teaspoon edible red food coloring

Vegetables:
8 ounces baby mushrooms
8 ounces cherry tomatoes
1 large red bell pepper, cut into 1-inch cubes
1 medium fresh pineapple, peeled, cored, and cut into 1-inch cubes

1. Place the tofu cubes into a medium-size bowl. In another small bowl, stir together the sugar and boiling water until the sugar dissolves. Then stir in the remaining ingredients (except the vegetables). Cool slightly for about 10 minutes.
2. Pour the mixture over the tofu, stirring to coat it evenly. Set it aside at room temperature for 2 hours, stirring several times. Lift the tofu carefully from the marinade, allowing the excess liquid to drain off. Reserve the liquid.
3. Preheat the barbecue or grill. Thread tofu, pineapple, and vegetables alternately onto skewers. Grill the skewers for about 8 minutes, turning and basting several times with reserved marinade until crisp and cooked. Serve on a bed of shredded lettuce.
    Enjoy.
    Note: To prevent the wooden skewers from burning, soak them in water for 1 hour prior to using.

[Cook's Note]

One of my absolute favorite desserts is chocolate mousse. But I'm not a fan of light, airy chocolate mousse. I like mine thick, rich, and decadent—really naughty. If you're going to indulge in something this good, why not do it right? For years I've messed around with different recipes for this delicious dessert. Eventually I came up with this one, which, just like my Crème Brûlée, will remain a steadfast favorite among my recipes. Although it's a little fussy, the mousse is not that difficult to make and doesn't require many ingredients.

You may need an extra hour on the treadmill after this one, but believe me it's worth it.

Daisy's Chocolate Mousse

⅓ cup heavy cream
7 ounces bittersweet chocolate, chopped
3 teaspoons Grand Marnier or Cointreau (optional)
4 extra-large free-range eggs, separated
1 tablespoon soft brown sugar
1 tablespoon fine white sugar

1. In a heatproof bowl that sits snugly over a saucepan of simmering water (don't let the base of the bowl touch the simmering water), add the cream and the chocolate. Stir until the chocolate is completely melted and smooth. Remove the bowl from the saucepan, stir in the Grand Marnier, and set aside.
2. In a medium heatproof bowl, whisk the egg yolks with 1 tablespoon water and the brown sugar for 2 minutes. Place the bowl over the saucepan of simmering water and continue to whisk for another 2 to 3 minutes (making sure the eggs don't scramble).
3. Remove the bowl from the heat and whisk with an electric mixer on high speed for about 4 to 5 minutes, until the egg mix resembles whipped cream. Set aside to cool.
4. Whisk the egg whites in a large chilled bowl until they become thick and form soft peaks. Add the white sugar and continue whisking until the egg whites become firm and form stiff peaks. *(Note: Before I mix the egg whites, I*

put a large bowl in the fridge for about 10 minutes to chill it. Then I wipe off any
condensation with a paper towel before adding the egg whites.)

5. Slowly and gently fold the egg yolk mix into the chocolate mix until it's evenly incorporated.

6. Add about one-third of the egg white mix to the chocolate mix and fold it in gently using a large metal spoon. Gently fold in the rest of the egg white mix in two batches until thoroughly combined.

7. Pour the mix into serving glasses or ramekins and chill for at least 1 hour before serving.

To serve, garnish with some candied orange peel or a segment of orange on top of a dollop of whipped cream.

Enjoy.

Chapter 8

Young Island to Mustique to Tobago Cays

Coordinates:Young Island 66 17'S 162 25'E, Mustique 12 52'N 61 11'W

Thursday, June 19

Oh, how I dread early starts! We rarely have time to grab breakfast before getting *Daisy* ready to head out. The sail from Young Island to Mustique was quite rough, with large swells and winds up to 35 knots. Captain Bob, Edi, and Justin manned the stations. Meanwhile, I adopted my usual horizontal position for most of the leg, squeezing the life out of the cushion. That's me: predictably useless and totally pathetic in anything other than perfect conditions. My overactive imagination was once again swinging from the mast and screaming, anticipating accidental jibes, broken booms, torn sails, and, of course, the dreaded "man overboard." Despite my silent predictions of doom, we arrived completely unscathed.

We arrived in Mustique just in time for lunch. Edi and Justin swam off the boat, while Bob went ashore to customs. As soon as Bob had cleared us in, we went ashore. I bought some lovely fresh vegetables from a tiny seafront market. The little stores were selling locally grown organic fruit and vegetables, many I'd never seen before. The friendly stall owner offered us a piece of soursop, which resembled nothing I'd ever eaten before. Edi said it tasted like warm vanilla ice cream with strawberry and banana notes. Delicious. There were also jackfruit, guava, sugar apple, and passion fruit (my favorite). Another unusual fruit is the cherimoya, also known as the custard apple because of its sherbet-like texture. The flesh is white, soft, and sweet but full of black seeds, about the size of orange pips. Mark Twain called it "the most delicious fruit known to man." The thing that always surprises me about this fruit is that it's rarely mentioned anywhere that the seeds are deadly poisonous if crushed. We skipped the cherimoya and bought passion fruit, mangos, and bananas.

Local fruit & veg vendor on Mustique

I couldn't resist the heavenly aroma of freshly baked bread that wafted from the local bakery. I bought a large loaf of crusty sourdough bread, still hot from the oven.

As I strolled back to the boat with my fresh purchases, I was reminded why Mustique was quickly becoming one of my favorite Caribbean islands. Mustique is a small 1,400-acre island that is privately owned by the shareholders of the Mustique Company, representing seventeen countries. This island is maintained under a strictly controlled development plan, with 100 private residences and 72 villas. The villas are available for weekly rental, but I warn you: they do not come cheap.

It was here a couple of years ago that I fulfilled my lifelong dream of horseback riding along a beach. Besides its magnificent beaches, this island's properties are maintained to the highest possible standards. It's no coincidence that royalty, film stars, and billionaires own homes here. You won't find ramshackle buildings with corrugated iron roofs, broken-down cars, craters in the road, or, in fact, any signs of poverty or neglect. The entire pristine island is groomed to perfection.

I had really looked forward to taking Edi and Justin for cocktails at Basil's bar, which is perched on stilts over the Caribbean Sea and has a far-reaching reputation as one of the world's best bars. Basil's is also home of the Mustique Blues Festival held January 27 through February 10. Unfortunately for us, Basil's was being refurbished, so the bar was closed for business. Disappointed, we returned to *Daisy*. To perk us up, I made some delicious sandwiches for lunch, tuna salad and fresh crab with tarragon and cream cheese on the freshly baked bread. After lunch we set sail for the Tobago Cays, arriving around 4:30 p.m. Edi and Justin decided to clean the hull of the boat while I made dinner. In a beautiful spot like the Tobago Cays, with its crystal clear, bath temperature water, cleaning the hull of a boat isn't all that unpleasant of a job.

After dinner we drank cocktails and played Balderdash. We all enjoy board games, especially with a couple of cocktails! We made plans to go snorkeling the next day. The first and last time we were in the Cays (one of the best vacations I've ever had), we were on a charter boat. I clearly remember how fantastic the snorkeling was. The water is very shallow and a deeper turquoise than you can possibly imagine.

Friday, June 20

We awoke to a cheerless, miserable morning. We peered through the hatch to see a heavy gray tropical haze all around. It didn't look promising for our planned snorkel. We all watched with deepening disappointment as more clouds rolled in along with boatloads of tourists from neighboring islands.

To cheer us up, I made a special breakfast of Raspberry, Banana, and Passion Fruit Stuffed French Toast with warmed maple syrup. Bob, Edi, and Justin took the dinghy over to one of the little islands to try and snorkel. Meanwhile, I stayed on board to tidy the boat and do some laundry. The boys didn't stay out for long: the drizzle had quickly turned to heavy rain, and the wind was blowing with increasing strength. It was churning up the seabed, making visibility impossible, so they gave up snorkeling and returned to *Daisy*.

We retreated below deck and closed up the boat. After lunch I got out my acrylic paints, and despite the wind and the rain hammering the decks above, I spent a very relaxing afternoon painting while the boys read and Bob worked on his computer. The rain continued all day long, so I decided to make a special dinner to boost morale.

I prepared delicious Mushroom Risotto, followed by a dessert of Passion Fruit, Kiwi, and Mango Trifle. It had been a quiet, pleasant, and restful day after all, despite the dreadful weather.

The Tobago Cays are a group of tiny uninhabited islands sheltered by a horseshoe reef. In an attempt to protect the delicate reef, the St. Vincent government declared the islands a marine park. The waters here are exceptionally clear and boast a diverse selection of marine life. This attracts thousands and thousands of tourists to the area each year. The only way to reach these islands is by boat. Unfortunately, the delicate coral reefs have sustained damage over the last few years due to so many of the visiting boats anchoring carelessly. A few moorings have been placed here, but not nearly enough to cope with the demand. It's asking a lot of one small, economically strapped nation to efficiently protect this beautiful area. In order to prevent further damage to this magnificent coral reef, we as visitors can easily take a few simple precautions to aid in its protection:

- Don't drop anchors, either boat or dinghy, near the coral.
- Do take a little longer to locate a sandy or grassy area for anchoring.
- Don't stand on or touch the coral.
- Don't remove shells or coral from the seabed.

Coral only grows about one inch every twenty years, and while the reefs look sturdy, their surface is composed of many tiny, vulnerable creatures. Most of the damage to coral reefs is not done solely by the anchor but by the chain dragging across the reef as the wind shifts the boat from side to side.

Protecting the reefs may mean anchoring farther away than we would like, but if everyone made this small effort, the reefs would survive for years to come and be there for many others to enjoy in the future.

Raspberry, Banana, and Passion Fruit Stuffed French Toast

¾ cup fresh raspberries plus ¼ cup for garnish

3 passion fruits, pulp and seeds

1 banana, thinly sliced

4 tablespoons unsalted butter, softened, divided

8 slices thick white bread or brioche

3 large free-range eggs

2 tablespoons heavy cream

⅓ cup confectioners' sugar (or icing sugar)

1. **To make the filling:** In a medium bowl, mix together the raspberries, passion fruits, and banana; set aside.
2. **To make the French toast:** Using half the butter, spread on each slice of bread. Spread the fruit over four of the buttered slices, then place the remaining slices on top, butter side down.
3. In a medium bowl beat the eggs together with the cream, then add the confectioners' sugar; stir to mix.
4. Heat the remaining butter in a frying pan. Dip the sandwiches carefully into the egg mix, then into the frying pan. Fry for about 2 minutes per side.
5. Remove the sandwiches from the pan and blot on kitchen paper towels.
6. Cut the sandwiches in half and dredge with confectioners' sugar.
   Garnish with some fresh raspberries and serve.
   Enjoy.

[Cook's note]

Eating risotto always takes me straight back to Tuscany. This dish is real Italian comfort food—wonderful on a cold winter's night served with a lovely Italian red wine.

Mushroom Risotto

3 cups chicken or vegetable stock
3 tablespoons olive oil
3 large shallots, finely chopped
2 celery stalks, finely chopped
1 cup uncooked Arborio rice
½ cup dry white wine
1 teaspoon ground coriander
Salt and pepper
8 ounces mixed mushrooms, cleaned and sliced
2 tablespoons mascarpone or crème fraîche
1 tablespoon fresh herbs, chopped
2 tablespoons Parmesan, freshly grated

1. In a medium saucepan, bring the stock to a boil, then reduce to a simmer.
2. Heat 1 tablespoon olive oil in a deep sauté pan; add the shallots and sauté for 2 to 3 minutes until softened but not browned. Add the celery and cook for another 2 minutes. 3. Gradually stir in the rice; cook for another 2 minutes. Pour in the wine and cook until it has been absorbed, about 3 to 4 minutes. Add a ladleful (about a half cup) of the hot stock with the coriander and cook, stirring, until the liquid has been absorbed.
4. Continue to add the stock, a ladleful at a time, allowing each addition to be absorbed before adding more, until the rice is al dente (cooked but firm to the bite). The risotto should be very moist and creamy. Season with salt and pepper to taste.
5. Heat the remaining oil in a sauté pan, add the sliced mushrooms, and cook and stir until softened. Stir through the risotto. Add the mascarpone or crème fraîche; stir well.

To serve: Divide the risotto among warm plates. Sprinkle with herbs and Parmesan, and serve with slices of freshly baked warm baguette.

Enjoy.

Passion Fruit, Kiwifruit, and Mango Trifle

4 ripe mangos, peeled and diced small
4 kiwifruits, peeled and thinly sliced
8 passion fruits
4 cups heavy cream
¼ cup sugar
Store-bought shortcake (or sponge cake)
Cointreau liqueur

1. Place the mangos and kiwifruit slices into a medium bowl. Put a strainer over the bowl.
   Put the pulp, seeds, and the juice from 6 passion fruits into the strainer; set aside the other 2 passion fruits for later.
2. Allow all the juice to drain from the passion fruit.
3. Pour the heavy cream and sugar into a medium bowl and using a hand mixer, whisk to stiff peaks. This will take a couple of minutes.
4. Slice the shortcake and drizzle each slice with Cointreau, about 1 teaspoon per slice.
5. In a wine or sundae glass, layer the ingredients: start with the shortcake, then fruit, then cream, and so on until you reach the top.
   To serve: Top with cream and the seeds from the 2 remaining passion fruits. Enjoy.

Chapter 9
Tobago Cays to Grenada

Coordinates: Tobago Cays 12 38'N 61 21W; Grenada, St. George's 12 03'N 61 45'W

Saturday, June 21

We set sail very early for our trip down to Grenada, weighing anchor at dawn. With huge swells and 30-knot winds gusting to 50, sailing was definitely not a pleasant experience, especially for yours truly. My overactive imagination was in full-panic mode, and I was frozen to my spot under the dodger. It was too rough to go below, so I stayed glued to my seat. The guys didn't seem at all concerned, and this should have calmed me. But, sadly, nothing short of a bottle of vodka would have taken the edge off my fear at this particular time.

As the morning wore on and we continued our journey south, the weather cleared and the wind dropped to a much calmer 20 to 30 knots. We enjoyed another special encounter with our dolphin friends; happily, they were becoming a very familiar sight, and I welcomed the distraction.

We approached the Grenada coastline around 3 p.m. and continued on around the coast to the southern end of the island to look for a suitable bay for the night. We finally dropped anchor in a secluded little bay at Martin's Marina, and having secured *Daisy*, we all went ashore to hire a car and drive around the island. We stopped en route to pick up some provisions, just a few groceries and some more beer. We were currently suffering from "the great beer crisis," as our stocks on board had become sadly depleted. Before returning to *Daisy,* we dropped in to Martin's bar for a drink. Bob worked on his computer while Ed, Justin, and I kicked back with some cocktails. We didn't linger long at Martin's because, unfortunately, the bar was swarming with mosquitoes. Quite obviously word was out among the mosquito community that I had arrived. Wherever I go they find me—they rarely bother Bob. I've decided that it's because I'm so hot blooded. I've suffered from hot flashes for years, and I'm told mosquitoes are drawn to heat. As women tend to project more heat than men, they get bitten more often. (I've no idea if that's true, but it makes sense to me.)

Bob granted me a night off galley duty and took us all out to dinner. We found a local Chinese restaurant just a five-minute drive from the marina. As much as I love to cook, it made a pleasant change to eat out. The food was delicious and everyone was in good spirits.

Sunday, June 22

After a scrummy breakfast of banana-stuffed French toast and fresh fruit, we went ashore to drive out around the coastline and look for a summer home for *Daisy*. We found Le Phare Bleu, a brand-new, beautiful little marina and resort that was still partially under construction. We met with the contractor and Janni, one of the resort owners. They were both very welcoming, friendly, and helpful. Bob asked about the hurricane plans for the boats in the marina. The bay appeared secluded and well protected, and it seemed well thought out. Mooring balls were strategically placed in the bay in preparation for hurricane season. While Bob talked with Janni and the contractor, Edi, Justin, and I checked out the rest of the resort. There was a lovely swimming pool and sundeck overlooking the bay next to the bar. At the end of the dock was a light ship housing a resident's lounge with comfortable oversized sofas, a good selection of DVDs available for loan, and stacks of books and magazines. There were five individual, clean, spacious showers and restrooms. The light ship also had a fabulous a la carte restaurant. Conveniently, also on-site were a small grocery store, yacht service, and marine and electrical engineer service. *(Since we were last there, a customs office has opened for check-in. For more information about the businesses on-site, see Appendix 4: Helpful Websites).*

Edi and Justin on the lightship.

After inspecting the docks and looking around the resort, we left to explore all the other marinas, which only confirmed what we had originally thought: Le Phare Bleu was where we wanted to be. We spent the rest of the afternoon getting *Daisy* ready as quickly as possible; the wind was starting to pick up, and we wanted to get her situated in Le Phare Bleu before nightfall. The sea was quite rough as we motored around, with high winds once again. The boat dipped and swayed as we made our way. Edi drove the car back to meet us on the dock. It was not the easiest docking, with the strong winds blowing us all over the place, but we managed it eventually, thanks to *Daisy*'s bow thrusters. Captain Bob had become quite proficient at maneuvering *Daisy* in difficult conditions.

Once alongside, I set about tidying the boat. It felt so good to know I'd be staying put for a few months.

Monday, June 23

I took a leisurely early-morning swim before breakfast. After my swim, I showered on the light ship and then went back to make breakfast for my still soundly sleeping crew. After breakfast I went up to the bar and snuggled in one of the lovely deep couches. I sipped delicious cappuccino while I worked on my journal.

Both Bob and I kept busy with boat chores all morning, servicing the water-maker and doing laundry while the boys went for a swim. We ate lunch at the bar and then drove into town to the customs office to check in. Once we were officially cleared in, we drove out to explore some of the coastline villages. The colors on this island were amazing; the local people paint everything in vibrant colors, including the tires that line the sides of the road. Boulders and rocks were all brightly painted, and some had messages on them, such as directions and distances to other villages. All of the houses, from the smallest ramshackle building to the most elaborate mansion, were painted red, yellow, green, and blue. Many of the larger houses boasted large verandas with grand balustrades and gardens bursting with tropical flowers and trees.

We seemed to attract quite a bit of attention from the locals: most visitors to the island tend to keep to the local attractions, such as the beaches and tourist spots; consequently, the four of us stood out as we passed through the villages, which were bustling with people rushing to and fro. There were children playing in the street, people shopping, and groups of men sitting around smoking. As we drove through one village, we passed a group of locals gathered on a street corner. They smiled and waved at us as we passed by, and we all waved back with a great display of enthusiasm. Realizing we had missed our turning, we turned around and drove back through the village, again passing the group on the corner. They smiled and waved at us once again, and we returned the smiles with exaggerated, enthusiastic waving.

About a mile down the road, Edi said, "The turning must be back through the village, Dad." So we turned around and drove back through the village for the third time. This time the group on the corner waved at us but with looks of confusion rather than smiles. Our map was no help at all: the road we were on led to a dead end, so we turned around again. This was becoming ridiculous. As we passed the group for the fourth time, they all raised their hands in the air in confusion, as if to say "What the hell!" They didn't look at all amused, whereas the four of us were doubled over with laughter. We decided that right road or wrong road, we couldn't drive back through that village again.

Instead, we headed out along the coast road for a few miles and then up into the rain forest. The drive was exhilarating. As we climbed higher and higher, the road became narrower and narrower, until it was only a rough, rock-strewn lane, barely wide enough for our little car. Meeting and passing the occasional vehicle coming in the other direction was interesting to say the least. I was distracted by the beauty of the forest, which I found quite breathtaking; it was easy to see how Grenada earned its name of "Spice Island." We stopped to pick nutmeg and mangos, which hung heavily from the branches, as did oranges, papayas, and avocados. Banana, lime, and cocoa trees lined the sides of the road and filled the forest. Having grown up in England—where our garden consisted of the usual apples, plums, potatoes, tomatoes, and blackberries—I was excited to pick such luscious fruits and spices right at the side of the road.

The production of nutmeg has been the backbone of the island's economy and agriculture since 1843, when it was introduced to the island from India. In 2001 Grenada was the world's second-largest exporter of nutmeg. Then the Grenadian firms started exporting nutmeg at sixty percent higher than the average world export price, so by 2009 they slipped to the ninth-largest exporter.

We arrived back at the boat early in the evening. I made a very spicy curry for dinner. Unfortunately, I got carried away with the spices: the dish was so hot, I couldn't even eat it (and I didn't include that recipe in this book). My red-faced boys, however, managed to clean their plates—with the help of a few bottles of beer to wash it all down. Exhausted from our busy day, after dinner everyone just crashed.

Bob was due to return to America the next morning for a few weeks' work. I felt fortunate to have my boys Edi and Justin to keep me company for a little longer yet. I knew I was going to miss them both terribly when they left.

Over the next couple of days, the boys and I quickly made friends with the resort staff and the other yachties staying at the marina. We played cards at the bar each night with Angela and Steve, a couple Edi and Justin had become friendly with. Like us, they stayed on their boat as resort residents. Justin and Edi also quickly became friends with Rudell and Kyle, the guys behind the bar, even enjoying a couple of lads' nights out on the town with them.

One evening a few days after Bob had returned to the States, Edi, Justin, and I played cards with our friends as usual. I had returned to the boat before the boys. When I woke at around 2 a.m. to get a drink of water, I peeked into their cabins and noticed they hadn't returned. So I got dressed and walked up to the bar, expecting to find them there, possibly passed out on the comfy sofas. The bar was dark and there was no one around, so I walked up to the security gate to ask the guard if he had seen them. "Oh yes, Miss Daisy, they went out with Rudell and Kyle just a few hours ago," he informed me cheerfully, showing his wide, toothless grin. "Don't you worry, Miss Daisy, Rudell and Kyle will take good care of them—they'll be back soon," he laughed. I wasn't so sure.

Back at the boat, I couldn't sleep. I just couldn't help worrying. Even though the boys are adults (well, most of the time), Grenada is not a safe place at night. And it was now approaching 3 a.m. I got dressed again and walked back up to the security guard. Still no sign of them. I reluctantly returned to the boat. There was little I could do, but I knew I wouldn't sleep until they came home. Back on board, I went below and made tea. With my cup of tea and a cookie in hand, I went back up on deck to sit and wait for them. From my seat under the dodger, I could clearly see down the dock to the road that led to the resort. I quietly sipped my tea with Nicho-San by my side, watching and hoping to see headlights. My mind was turning cartwheels worrying about them. Suddenly I noticed that Nicho-San was leaning out of the cockpit, watching something on the dock. I leaned forward past the cover of the dodger to see what he was looking at, and to my great relief there they were! Ed and Justin, flat out sleeping on the dock. They must have staggered back to the boat while I was below making tea. I was then worried about them rolling off the dock into the water, so I tried to wake them. It would have been easier to wake the dead. Gentle prodding turned into slapping, but still they didn't move. So I threw a bucket of water over them. Ed stirred and mumbled something unrepeatable, but Justin remained motionless. I tried to pick them up and drag them onto the boat, but that was a complete waste of time. Realizing that they weren't moving anywhere, I gave up and went back to bed. The morning dawned to find Edi and Justin wondering why their clothes were wringing wet when it obviously hadn't rained. I wasn't about to enlighten them. I just smiled and made them some strong coffee.

In the days after Bob left, we became friendly with Max, the resort's chef. One night he overheard our conversation about our love for curry, which wasn't on the Le Phare Bleu menu. Max said he would be happy to make it for us, and so he did. From that day on, Max would regularly make us curry on demand; in fact, he made anything we requested as long as he had the ingredients on hand. His delicious curry remained my favorite.

One evening Steve and Angela introduced Edi and me to Mexican Train, a game of dominos. We were instantly hooked. After our introduction to the game, we got together most nights to play.

The evenings at Le Phare Bleu, drinking buckets of the local beer and playing Mexican Train into the early hours with my friends, are some of my favorite Caribbean memories.

It got pretty lonely on the boat after Edi and Justin left, so I decided to take a trip home. In late June, I returned to the mainland for a couple of weeks. I decided against taking Nicho-San back with me, because all the traveling would have been too stressful for him. Angela and Steve kindly offered to take care of him until my return to St. George's and Le Phare Bleu.

Lettuce Wraps

1½ cups chicken, diced (or soy crumbles)
2 tablespoons white mushrooms, finely chopped
2 tablespoons water chestnuts, finely chopped
Salt and pepper
Pinch of sugar
2 teaspoons lite soy sauce
2 teaspoons rice wine or dry sherry
Pinch of red pepper flakes
2 teaspoons cornstarch
2 to 3 tablespoons toasted sesame oil
2 teaspoons fresh ginger, finely chopped
3 teaspoons scallions, finely chopped
2 tablespoons Szechuan preserved vegetables, finely chopped
2 tablespoons oyster sauce
1 teaspoon pure honey
12 crisp romaine lettuce leaves, to serve

1. Mix the chicken or soy crumbles with the mushrooms, water chestnuts, salt and pepper, sugar, soy sauce, rice wine or dry sherry, red pepper flakes, and cornstarch. Blend until all the ingredients are thoroughly combined.
2. Heat the oil in a wok over a medium heat. Add the ginger and scallions, followed by the chicken or soy crumbles. Stir-fry for 1 minute.
3. Add the Szechuan vegetables and cook and stir for 1 minute.
4. Add the oyster sauce and honey; blend well and cook for 1 minute. Transfer to a warmed serving dish. Serve the lettuce leaves on a separate plate.
   To serve: Put 2 to 3 tablespoons of the mix on a leaf and roll it tightly to form a small package; eat with your fingers.
   Enjoy.

[Cook's note]
Vegetable couscous makes a great complementary side dish.

Roasted Striped Bass and Shrimp in Pernod

2 tablespoons olive oil
1 cup yellow onion, chopped
2 ounces pancetta or bacon, finely diced
1 tablespoon garlic, chopped
1 (28-ounce) can plum tomatoes, drained and diced
1 teaspoon saffron threads, soaked in 1 tablespoon water
1 teaspoon Maldon sea salt flakes
½ teaspoon freshly ground black pepper
½ cup dry white wine
¼ cup Pernod
1 2- to 3-pound striped bass fillet, skin removed
1½ pounds uncooked large shrimp, shelled and deveined
2 tablespoons fresh flat-leaf parsley, chopped
1 lime, cut into 6 wedges

1. Preheat oven to 350 degrees F.
2. Heat the oil in a medium sauté pan; sauté the onion and pancetta or bacon over medium heat for 10 minutes, or until the onion is translucent.
3. Add the garlic, tomatoes, saffron, salt, pepper, white wine, and Pernod; simmer over medium heat for 5 minutes.
4. Place the fish in a rectangular baking dish. Pour the sauce over the fish. Bake uncovered for 20 minutes or until the fish is cooked through. Add the shrimp and cook for another 3 to 4 minutes, until the shrimp is cooked through.
5. Sprinkle with the chopped parsley and a lime wedge, and serve.
   This dish is good served either hot or at room temperature.
   Enjoy.

[Cook's Note]

This is so good, so simple, and a favorite with absolutely everyone I serve it to. It doesn't require many ingredients or preparation time. It's unfussy, yet tastes like something you would order in a fine dining establishment.

Poached Pears in Red Wine

1 bottle red wine
6 large, firm pears, peeled (with stems on)
½ cup brown sugar
2 cinnamon sticks
4 whole cloves

1. Pour the red wine into a saucepan large enough to stand the pears upright in.
2. Add the brown sugar, cinnamon sticks, and cloves; bring slowly to a boil.
3. Turn off the heat; place the pears carefully upright in the pan, with only the stems out of the liquid.
4. Marinate for 1 hour.
5. Bring the liquid back to a boil. Lower the heat and simmer gently for 30 minutes until the pears are tender but not soft.
6. Leave the pears standing in the liquid for an hour or longer before serving. Serve warm or cold with a dollop of whipped cream.
   Enjoy.

Chapter 10

The Journey Continues— Grenada to Los Testigos

Coordinates: Los Testigos 11 22' 59"N 63 05' 50"W

Tuesday, July 29

Following a couple of weeks back on dry land, it was time to go back to to Grenada and *Daisy*. My return trip to Grenada was a nightmare, taking a full twenty-nine hours door-to-door, with cancellations that brought about an unplanned overnight stop in St. Lucia and some rather unpleasant arguments with airline staff. For once, I was very happy that Nicho-San wasn't traveling with me.

I remember the days when traveling was actually fun. It was easy and totally stress-free: You could just buy a ticket and jump on a plane, carrying whatever you wanted. You could even check as many bags as you liked without incurring all the expensive extra charges.

Travel is anything but fun these days. There is a great amount of stress inflicted upon the traveler—stress brought about through all the airport security. Yes, I do realize increased security is very necessary today, but it's still exhausting. As the innocent traveler passing through layers and layers of airport security today, you are made to feel much like a prison inmate. You and the other weary passengers are rounded up and marched in long lines that snake around the airport, Disney-style, all shuffling along with bags and screaming children in tow. Uniformed security staff shout instructions, lording their power like prison guards marching prisoners to their cells.

Once you've removed shoes, hats, coats, belts, and jewelry; emptied your pockets of keys, phones, and coins; and removed the Mac from its case (and wished you hadn't worn the underwire bra), you tiptoe barefoot through the X-ray machine, which always beeps (probably because of the underwire bra) and probably emits damaging radiation, doing God-only-knows-what to your body. Then you're subjected to standing arms out while some buxom, stern-faced, uniformed wench runs her rubber gloves over your body and up your skirt. Then you attempt to collect your belongings that are piling up at the end of the conveyor belt and are probably being grabbed by security for extra checks because you left a forgotten tube of toothpaste in the bottom of the bag.

(I'm always thoroughly exhausted and horribly sweaty before I even begin the marathon trek to the departure gate, which has more often than not been changed to another terminal that's at least thirty minutes' walk from the original gate. I've yet to board a plane while not in a sweaty, horrible mess. All attempts at nice hair and perfectly applied makeup are totally blown out the window.)

Once you're finally on board, you discover that the exit aisle seat the ticketing agent promised to reserve is, in fact, the middle seat near the back of the plane, nowhere near the exit aisle but right next to the toilet. All the overhead bins are full, so you have to stuff your carry-on under your seat, giving you no legroom at all. Then you find you're sitting squished between two fat people who fart and who have put up both arm rests so they can spread out over your seat, too, leaving you absolutely no room to move. The person seated in front of you leans the seat all the way back, so you're now wedged in between two hot, smelly bodies with your nose pressed up against the back of a seat.

Then—just in case the unhelpful ticketing agents, airport security, gate changes, and bad seating assignment aren't enough to stretch your tolerance level to the limit—you discover that the small child sitting behind you thinks it's great fun to kick the crap out of the back of your seat and bang the tray table up and down because she likes the noise it makes. Just when you think the child might settle down, she starts screaming at the top of her lungs for the entire rest of the trip. These are just a few of the joyous delights of airline travel (in coach).

At 10 a.m., after nearly thirty hours of travel, I finally arrived at Le Phare Bleu and was so warmly greeted by everyone; the cab driver must have thought

I was a celebrity. I was exhausted but very happy to be back. It almost felt like coming home.

Wednesday, July 30, through Sunday, August 10

For the next twelve days, while I waited for Bob and Danni to arrive, I kept myself busy with boat chores—cleaning, polishing, varnishing, and baking—in preparation for the upcoming trip to Los Testigos. I wanted to make sure we had a clean boat and plenty of delicious food on board. My nights, which were much more fun, were spent at the bar playing Mexican Train with my friends.

Monday, August 11

After another very tiring trip, Bob and Danni arrived safely at Le Phare Bleu late Sunday evening. I was so happy to see them both. After ten days alone, I was really missing my family. Bob and I introduced Danni to everyone, grabbed a quick drink, and returned to *Daisy* for a good night's sleep.

We spent a quiet day relaxing and sipping cocktails by the pool, just doing simple jobs around the boat in preparation for our trip. The evening was spent at the bar with our friends, enjoying the Oil Down on the beach. (No, Oil Down isn't a free-for-all with a giant bottle of suntan oil, in case that's what you're thinking.) Oil Down is a traditional Grenada dish that's served on special occasions. Similar to a stew, it's made with local vegetables, fish, chicken, pork, and beef. I thought it was a little like a thick winter stew made by someone who couldn't decide which ingredients to use, so they used everything. Everyone appeared to be enjoying the stew and watching the festivities that celebrate the start of the Grenada Carnival. The party on the beach was a lot of fun.

After the beach party, we found a quiet table at the back of the bar away from the crowds, where we sat with another small group of people also planning on making the crossing to Los Testigos. After much discussion regarding our route, the decision was made to avoid not only mainland Venezuela but also Isla Margarita. There had been many recent reports of piracy in and around Porlamar; it seemed foolish to put ourselves at risk when it could so easily be avoided. We planned to travel directly from Hog Island, Grenada, to Los Testigos, where we intended to spend a few days before sailing directly on to La Blanquilla.

When reviewing the charts, I had planned for us to stop at Isla La Orchila on our way to Los Roques. Bob pointed out that La Orchila is a military base and must be avoided by at least 5 miles. With the changes made and our forthcoming route decided upon, we were free to relax and enjoy the Grenada Carnival, which we were looking forward to attending the next day.

Tuesday, August 12

In the early afternoon, a cab picked up a group of us from the marina. We then made the short twenty-minute drive into St. George's, the capital of Grenada, where we spent the afternoon watching the carnival procession. Everyone was in party spirits: adults, children, locals, and tourists alike all joined in the fun.

We had deliberately delayed our departure so we could experience the carnival, one of the island's largest annual festivals, and I'm glad we did. Months and months of hard work go into the carnival preparations, which are linked to the French, British, African, and Caribbean heritage and are brimming with pageantry. All the local people and even the tourists throw themselves wholeheartedly into carnival spirit. The Grenada Carnival is something I would highly recommend watching or even taking part in if you don't mind getting "down and dirty."

Many carnival participants adopt the disguises of Shortknee or Jab Jab. The traditional Shortknee costume evolved from Grenadian history and combines masks and colorful costumes with mirrors attached to reflect enemies, and ankle bells to make music. Talcum powder is sprinkled on people who give cash to the carnival participants as a sign of appreciation. What a fantastic spectacle.

The festivities begin in July, but true carnival week starts at the beginning of August with the J'ouvert, an integral part of the carnival tradition that has many influences dating back from the emancipation from slavery in 1838. Participants and spectators alike smear themselves all over with paint, mud, engine oil, tar, stale molasses, or creosote; it's incredibly messy and smelly. Picture this combined with the talcum powder sprinkled by the Jab Jab and Shortknee participants, and you can imagine how messy this carnival can become. We had been warned of the possible mess, so we had wisely picked a balcony at one of the hotels, overlooking the streets, where we enjoyed a bird's-eye view of the procession at a safe distance.

The traditional Jab Jab or Devil Mas bands that emerge at nightfall to parade through the town are what I found the scariest of all. (Jab means "devil.") They smear themselves totally black with engine oil (or whatever) and wear little more than their red-horned helmets. They're designed to terrify onlookers with their grotesque appearance and weird dances, and they do.

Traditional authentic Jab music consists of blowing conch shells, drumming, and chanting, pretty much the way it was done originally by the African slaves. Huge crowds of onlookers and tourists gather to watch the procession through the streets of St. George's, and it quickly becomes one enormous party—people often dance until they fall over.

Wednesday, August 13

So many last-minute jobs needed doing before we could leave. It was back to the nail-biting, panic-stricken, rush-to-finish routine. Poor Danni was sick, and we ended up having to take her to the local hospital. After several hours and a few tests, it was confirmed that everything was OK, so there was no need to delay our departure. We finished our preparations, said good-bye to our friends at Le Phare Bleu, and motored quietly out of the marina just after five in the evening. I felt as though I was leaving home.

We sailed around the head to Prickly Bay, where we dropped anchor among the three other boats that we were sailing with. I'm always much happier when sailing with other boats. The waters around the Venezuelan coastline can be very dangerous for lone boats, which become easy targets for pirates, particularly if they sail close to the mainland. Our plan was to say at least 40 miles off the coast. Many of the pirates/thieves use small motorboats, so they're limited to how far they can travel from the mainland. If you're far enough out, they won't be able to reach you.

For dinner I made my Sesame Noodles with Shrimp and Cilantro, followed by a refreshing Citron Fromage. Then we worked until midnight, finishing last-minute tasks, such as stowing everything, completing a few repairs, and checking the generator and engine.

Thursday, August 14

At 1 a.m. we were the last of the group to leave the bay (nothing new there), but *Daisy* was quite a bit faster than the others, so we had no problem catching up. Because the leg from Grenada to Los Testigos could take between twelve to fifteen hours, we planned our departure so we would arrive in daylight. These islands do not have harbor lights, so arriving somewhere you have never been before in the dark is both dangerous and scary. Whenever possible, we plan our trips to arrive in daylight.

During the entire trip we had to go slow to stay with the fleet. Bob was concerned about running the engine so slowly, but unless we wanted to leave them all behind we had no choice. *Daisy* was speedy, even with her shoal draft. I was thoroughly enjoying the peaceful journey: warm air, light breezes, calm seas.

Daniela and I took the 3 a.m. watch; Bob took over at 6:30 a.m. This was our first night crossing since leaving Virgin Gorda in the British Virgin Islands; all our other legs had been day sails. At night everyone must take their turn on deck watching for other boats, monitoring the instruments, and watching for changing weather conditions. Our night crossing from Virgin Gorda to St. Maarten had been managed by Edi and Bob.

After breakfast we raised the sails and turned off the engine. It was a really beautiful morning, with bright blue skies, calm seas, and around 7 to 9 knots of wind—not much, but in the right direction and enough for us to maintain a steady 5 knots of speed. Daniela put out the fishing line, although she didn't manage to catch anything. We had hoped to catch a tuna, but I don't think we had the right lure; having said that, I don't think I would recognize the right lure if it was put in front of me. (I made a mental note to learn more about fishing.)

Later, while Danni and Bob napped and I was on watch, I was surprised and delighted to see two false killer whales swimming alongside *Daisy* and gracefully leaping out of the water. This was my first sighting of these magnificent creatures and I was thrilled. At one point they both leaped out of the water right alongside the cockpit. In one surreal moment as I stood at the helm, the two whales actually made eye contact with me before diving below and swimming off.

A false killer whale has a long, slender head and slim body, they are quite a bit larger than your average dolphin, and can grow up to nineteen feet in length. Their dorsal fin is prominent and curved back. They have unique flippers which have a prominent hump resembling an elbow halfway along the leading edge of each flipper. The false killer whale is a fast acrobatic swimmer and usually acts more like a dolphin than a whale, and can appear quite playful. I have tried during my time living aboard to learn as much as possible about the marine life that surrounds me, and dolphins are definitely my favorite species.

As we approached the islands of Los Testigos, large flocks of frigate birds and boobies flew overhead, fishing in the water around us. Frigate birds, which can have a wingspan of up to seven feet, don't fish like most seabirds: they carefully scoop fish from the water's surface without getting wet. They're unable to dive for their catch like other birds, and if they should accidentally end up in the water, they would probably drown, because they're completely unable to take off should they become submerged. Unlike other seabirds, the frigate's feathers don't have oil, so if the feathers become wet, they become heavy and cling to the body, making it impossible for the bird to take off. I read a fascinating account of a reported sighting: When a frigate bird had accidently landed on the water, two other frigate birds each took a wing and lifted the distressed bird out of the water and back into the air, carrying it until it was able to resume flight.

The frigate's water aversion explains why their general method of feeding is by stealing fish from other birds. They've often been seen catching a bird by its tail and shaking it mercilessly until it drops its catch. Female frigate birds are recognized by their white throats, while the males appear totally black but actually have a bright red throat that they blow up like a huge red balloon when attempting to attract a mate.

As we approached the islands we spotted several fishermen in their colorful boats. The little boats were quite unusual: they were long and had very high bows. Until quite recently I had never even heard of the islands of Los Testigos, and I was excited to arrive somewhere so remote. I knew very little about the islands or their history, and I looked forward to exploring.

[Cook's note]

This is another dish that I put together after enjoying a lovely shrimp and noodle dinner in Savannah, Georgia. I couldn't wait to create my own version of this spectacular dish. Fresh shrimp make a big difference, but frozen (raw) will do if fresh isn't available.

Sesame Noodles with Shrimp and Cilantro

2 cloves garlic, finely chopped
2 scallions, chopped
1 small fresh red chili pepper, seeded and sliced
1 bunch cilantro (set aside 1 tablespoon chopped cilantro for the garnish)
10 ounces fine egg noodles
2 tablespoons almond oil
2 teaspoons sesame oil
1 teaspoon shrimp paste
10 ounces shrimp, shelled and deveined (with tails removed)
2 tablespoons lime juice
2 tablespoons Thai fish sauce
1 teaspoon sesame seeds, toasted

1. Place the garlic, scallions, chili pepper, and cilantro in a mortar and pestle, and grind to a smooth paste.
2. Drop the noodles into a large pan of well-salted, boiling water and return to a boil; simmer for 4 minutes (or according to packet instructions).
3. Meanwhile, in a wok over medium heat, add the oils. When the oil is hot but not smoking, stir in the shrimp paste and ground garlic mixture; stir for 1 minute.
4. Add the whole shrimp and stir-fry for 2 minutes.
5. Stir in the lime juice and fish sauce; cook for another minute.
6. Drain but do not rinse the noodles; toss them into the wok with the shrimp. Sprinkle with the sesame seeds and chopped cilantro and serve at once. Enjoy.

[Cook's note]
A bit fussy but oh, so delicious and really worth the effort.

Citron Fromage

2 tablespoons water
1 level tablespoon powdered gelatin
3 large free-range eggs
Zest and juice of 2 large lemons, separated
½ cup (heaping) plus 1 tablespoon fine sugar
½ cup heavy cream
½ cup whipped cream and fresh mint leaves, for garnish

1. Place 2 tablespoons water in a small saucepan and sprinkle in the gelatin; soak for 5 minutes.
2. Separate the eggs, putting the yolks into a large bowl and the whites into another.
3. Finely grate the rind from the lemons and mix it into the egg yolks together with 1 tablespoon sugar.
4. Squeeze the lemons and strain the juice into the soaked gelatin. Place the saucepan over a low heat, stirring continuously. Do not allow it to boil. Immediately after the gelatin has dissolved, remove the pan from the heat.
5. Add ½ cup (heaping) sugar to the bowl of egg yolks. Whisk the egg yolks and sugar until pale and creamy. Slowly pour the dissolved gelatin into the egg mix, whisking all the time. Continue to whisk the mixture until it is cool and starting to thicken. In a separate small bowl, with a hand whisk lightly beat the heavy cream and fold into the mixture. Beat the egg whites until stiff, then fold them gently into the mix.
6. Spoon the mousse into individual glass dishes (wine glasses work well) and refrigerate for 1 hour.
   Add a dollop of whipped cream or pipe some whipped cream over each mousse, and add a mint leaf for garnish.
   Enjoy.

Chapter 11
Los Testigos

Coordinates: 11.3831 N, 63.0972W

We completed the leg from Grenada in thirteen and a half hours and arrived at Los Testigos in the early afternoon. The islands of Los Testigos are located 45 miles northeast of Juan Griego in Margarita and are the most remote of the Venezuela islands. The islands of Los Testigos are inhabited by a small group of interconnected families, around 160 people in all, who jealously protect the rich bounty of their islands. The islands are blessed with huge sand dunes, gorgeous beaches, and an abundance of fish and lobsters. There's only one way to get here and that's by boat; there are no ferries or airports. Los Testigos is the first group of islands to benefit from the Orinoco Delta runoff, so the islands are awash in open ocean swells and current.

The palm-fringed, white sandy beaches of the islands were doted with the colorfully painted fishing boats with high pointed bows; brightly painted small huts and little wooden buildings were lined behind the beach. Apart from the palms on the beach, the islands appeared very dry. There were a lot of cactus, scrub, and conifer-type trees and bushes covering the interior. The rocky outcrops were swarming with birds, pelicans, boobies, and frigates. Bob went across to the coast guard outpost with Rene (from *Gypsy Blues*) and Kriss (from *Spyglass*) to check in.

After customs we motored across to one of the neighboring islands where we all anchored together. Daniela and Bob went for a swim around the boat. The water here was actually quite clear and very clean, but because of the thick vegetation covering the seabed due to the runoff from the Venezuelan Orinoco River, it appeared very dark green.

In the evening we all went across to *Gypsy Blues* for cocktails and were joined by a Canadian family from the cat that sailed with us: Luci, John, and their two boys, Simi and Theo. We returned to our boat a couple of hours later for dinner. I made a frittata and green salad. Our only disappointment of the day was discovering that our satellite phone would not allow us to call out. Bob checked all the contracts and paperwork and everything appeared to be in order, but somehow someone somewhere screwed up, and we were left with no contact, other than the VHF and the SSB (single sideband radio).

Friday, August 15

I felt like I truly woke up in paradise, with wonderful blue sky, palm-fringed islands, crystal clear sea, and a gentle cooling breeze, slightly stronger than the day before. Bob took Danni ashore in the dinghy so she could go for a run along the beach; I stayed on board to do some cleaning and tidying. After breakfast we took *Whoops-a-Daisy* and followed Rene and Cheryl, fellow yachties from the sailboat *Gypsy Blues*, and Kriss from *Spyglass* to a small inlet where we anchored the dinghies and waded ashore. In order to reach the beach, we had to climb a very steep sand dune. Some of the dunes here reach 100 meters (328 feet) high. I thought I was going to die; my lungs felt as though they were about to explode. I was sweating profusely and had to stop every few steps to catch my breath. Between the suffocating heat, the steep slope, and the powdery soft sand slipping beneath my feet, it was a difficult climb to say the least. Once we reached the top, however, the view out across the ocean to the Venezuelan coastline in the distance was absolutely breathtaking.

I took a few minutes to enjoy the view and recover my composure, then we followed Kriss, Rene, and Cheryl along the wide, sandy path down to the shore. Iguana trails were everywhere, clearly marked in the sand. The beach that greeted us was one of the most beautiful I've ever seen. The sand resembled talcum powder, incredibly soft and white. It was very wide, sloping gently down to the shore where huge waves crashed upon it. I couldn't wait to get into the water.

The waves were strong and knocked me off my feet more than once, but it was a lot of fun. It was very difficult swimming against the current, but the crystal clear water was a wonderfully cool body temperature. It was hard to imagine a beach more perfect than this one.

Luci, John, and the boys were already there, surfing with their boogie boards. We all stayed and played in the surf for over an hour, taking silly photos with our waterproof cameras. We watched a couple of local fisherman pull a huge stingray out of the water not far from where we were swimming.

Danni attempted to ride the boogie board, sadly without too much success, but it was fun to watch. Everyone found it highly amusing when I once again got knocked over by a large wave, only to surface coughing and sputtering. It was all great fun and we could have happily stayed all day, but we realized our skin was starting to charcoal under the blistering sun. We needed to head back to the shade, so we quickly gathered our things from the beach and made our way back to the dinghy. The sand was so hot it was like walking on burning coals. Daniela's feet were burning through her flip-flops, so we made a dash for the shade of the trees at the foot of the dunes and then retreated to the beach where the dinghy awaited. The cool water felt so good on our scorched feet after the burning sand.

Once back on the boat, we enjoyed a lazy lunch of crab mousse with salad, crackers, corn and pepper salsa, and a couple of glasses of champagne. Lunch was followed by a wonderfully indulgent afternoon nap.

I was thoroughly enjoying not being invaded by flies and mosquitoes. My legs were finally beginning to heal, and the infuriating irritation had all but stopped—what bliss.

In the late afternoon Bob did some hull cleaning while Danni and I made snacks for the evening. We had invited everyone from our group of boats over for cocktails. I made a dish of sun-dried tomato hummus with pita chips, Gorgonzola and nut samosas, cheese and pineapple sticks, and crab mousse. Daniela made a delicious tomato salsa to serve with tortilla chips. Luci brought a selection of her delicious homemade sushi, and Cheryl brought popcorn for the boys. It was amazing what wonderful food we yachties could prepare in our tiny galleys. I haven't been to a house where such fabulous food was served. We had a lovely evening with great company and lively conversation. Sailors always have the best stories to tell. It had been another memorable day in paradise, definitely one for the journal.

Saturday, August 16

After breakfast we decided to move the boat around to another bay. Unfortunately, there was a problem with *Daisy*'s engine, and it took Bob about an hour to fix it before we were finally underway again, if only for a quick trip up the coast. We anchored next to four other boats in the bay, and the rest of our group joined us later in the afternoon.

Later we took *Whoops-a-Daisy* ashore, and Daniela, Rene, and Cheryl spotted a small shark off the far side of the sandy beach. It appeared to be a lemon shark, which are usually the most commonly sighted and, from my limited experience, seem quite shy and harmless (although I don't intend to put that theory to the test anytime soon). While we were swimming, we saw hundreds of large cushion starfish, also known as sea stars. I took photographs of Daniela holding one that was the size of a large dinner plate.

After our swim we walked to the rocky end of the island to admire the spectacular view. Danni and I laughed as Bob attempted to climb a palm tree. I wondered if maybe he was suffering from a little too much sun: climbing a palm tree isn't something he would normally do. Happily, I didn't think the coconuts were in any real danger. We collected some freshly fallen coconuts as well as some beautiful shells to take back to the boat with us.

Bob put the grill on for a quick dinner, but our barbecue refused to get hot (oh my, another job). It took us about an hour just to cook a few little kebabs. We may as well have been cooking over a lighted match.

Danni and a magnificent Cushion Starfish

That evening cocktails were on John and Luci's boat, and we really needn't have bothered cooking ourselves a dinner; Luci had put on a feast: chicken satay with peanut sauce, mini pizzas, fish cakes, and callaloo pancakes, all served with delicious and quite potent margaritas. We all drank and ate way too much, but we didn't stay very late because we were so tired. Luci proved to be an exceptional cook. I admired her ability to make so many mouth-watering dishes with only long-life provisions on board. She's amazing.

It had been another fun-filled, busy day with a couple of technical hiccups, but all ended well. As we motored *Whoops-a-Daisy* quietly back under a star-filled, moonlit sky, I felt blessed.

Sunday, August 17

We awoke to heavy rain, the first rain we had seen since leaving Grenada. Bob was very happy to have the rain wash all the salt water off *Daisy*. Fortunately, the storm didn't last long, and the heavy clouds were quickly replaced by blue sky and sunshine. Bob spent a couple of hours working with the SSB before he and Daniela went across to Rene's boat to try and send an e-mail to Edi. Daniela was worried about her horses back home. Bob needed Edi to contact our satellite provider and find out what the problem was. Because we had no Internet or satellite phone—in fact, no way of contacting anyone—we were grateful for Rene's help.

Not having any form of contact other than the SSB (which we were struggling to operate) was worrying us. Bob and Rene arranged a time to contact each other every day using the SSB so Rene could report on any reply he had received from Edi. I just hoped we could figure the damn thing out: trying to talk or hear anything on the SSB through the high-pitched crackle and screeching was seemingly impossible.

In the late afternoon, we motored back across to the bay we had visited the day before. We were planning to set sail for La Blanquilla, our next destination, either later that night or very early the next morning. We'd had a wonderful few days with our friends in these beautiful islands, and I was going to be sad to leave them.

Before dinner, Bob, Danni, and I went for one last swim in the Los Testigos waters. We then set about getting ready for our trip out. At 7:30 p.m. Bob and Daniela went ashore to look for leatherback turtles with Rene, Cheryl, John, Luci, and the boys. I stayed aboard: I had finally stopped itching and I did not want to risk getting any more mosquito bites. I put a movie on TV and watched from on deck while I waited for their return. Bob and Danni arrived back around 9 p.m. Apparently they had been too early to see the turtles, but Bob didn't want to stay any later because we were planning to leave in the early hours. We set the alarm for 1 a.m. so we could grab a couple hours of sleep.

Danni's Mango Salsa

1 medium red onion, diced small
2-inch piece fresh ginger, peeled and minced
2 tablespoons olive oil
2 cloves garlic, peeled and minced
3 ripe mangos, peeled, seeded, and diced small
⅓ cup freshly squeezed orange juice
2 teaspoons brown sugar
1 teaspoon Maldon sea salt flakes
½ teaspoon freshly ground black pepper
2 red jalapeno peppers, seeded and finely diced
2 tablespoons fresh cilantro leaves, minced

1. Cook the onion and ginger in the olive oil in a large sauté pan over medium-low heat for 10 minutes, or until the onions are translucent but not brown. Add the garlic and cook for 1 minute. Add the mangos, reduce heat to low, and cook and gently stir for 10 minutes.
2. Add the orange juice, brown sugar, salt, pepper, and jalapenos; cook for 10 minutes more, or until the orange juice is reduced, stirring occasionally.
3. Remove from the heat and add the cilantro.
   Serve warm or chilled.
   Enjoy.
   For pineapple salsa, simply follow the same recipe; omit the mango and add pineapple, diced small.

Sun-Dried Tomato Hummus

1 (14-ounce) can organic chickpeas, drained
8 sun-dried tomatoes (preferably oil-packed)
1 small red onion, peeled and roughly chopped
Juice of 1 lemon
3 tablespoons tahini paste
2 tablespoons olive oil plus extra for drizzling
3 cloves garlic, peeled and roughly chopped
2 tablespoons boiling water
¼ teaspoon Maldon sea salt flakes
Freshly ground black pepper

1. Put the chickpeas, sun-dried tomatoes, onion, and lemon juice in a blender; blend until smooth. Add the tahini paste, olive oil, and garlic; blend to thoroughly combine. Scrape down the sides of the blender, and add the boiling water.
2. Adjust salt and pepper to taste. Put the mixture in a small serving bowl and drizzle with olive oil.
   Serve with toasted pita bread.
   Enjoy.

[Cook's note]
These tasty little morsels are great served as an appetizer with predinner drinks.

Gorgonzola and Nut Samosas

½ cup onion, diced small
3 tablespoons butter
½ cup chopped apples (such as Granny Smiths)
½ cup mixed nuts (walnuts, pecans, and pine nuts), chopped and toasted
1 cup grated Parmesan
½ cup Panko breadcrumbs
2 cups Gorgonzola, crumbled
1 packet wonton wrappers (or spring roll wrappers)
Peanut oil, for deep-frying

1. In a large heavy-based pan, sauté the onions in the butter until translucent.
2. Add the apples, mixed nuts, Parmesan, and breadcrumbs; sauté for another minute.
3. Remove from the heat, let cool, then mix in the Gorgonzola.
4. Put a small amount of the filling in the middle of each wonton wrapper. Brush the wrapper edges with a little water and fold to make a triangle; press the edges together to seal.
5. Deep-fry for about 2 minutes or until golden brown. Drain on kitchen paper towels and serve warm.
   Enjoy.

Crab Mousse

8 to 10 ounces crabmeat (canned or fresh)
1 level tablespoon grated Parmesan
⅓ cup heavy cream
Salt and black pepper
½ teaspoon smoked paprika
Freshly squeezed juice of half a lemon
1 teaspoon lemon zest
5 fluid ounces aspic jelly
2 free-range eggs, whites only
Cucumber slices and cilantro leaves, for garnish

1. Use both the brown and white meat from the crab (if using canned crab, drain the crab into a strainer). Put the crabmeat, Parmesan, and cream into a liquidizer or blender, and buzz for 1 minute. Season with a little salt and freshly ground black pepper, smoked paprika, lemon juice, and lemon zest.
2. Prepare the aspic jelly according to the package directions and allow it to cool but not set. Add the aspic jelly to the crab mixture and stir well. Leave the mixture in a cool place until thick and cold.
3. Beat the egg whites until stiff but not dry, then fold them carefully into the crab mixture.
4. Turn the mousse into a mold or soufflé dish and leave to set in the refrigerator for at least 3 hours or overnight.
   Garnish the mousse with thin cucumber slices and cilantro leaves.
   Enjoy.

Chapter 12

Los Testigos to La Blanquilla and Los Roques

Coordinates: La Blanquilla 11 51' 12"N 64 35' 55"W, Los Roques 11 51' 27"N 66 45'27"W

Monday, August 18

The alarm woke us at 1 a.m., and by 1:30 a.m. we were underway. We had a full moon and calm seas but, unfortunately, not enough wind to sail, although we easily maintained an average 9 knots under motor. The trip across to La Blanquilla took just twelve hours; we arrived a little after 1 p.m. The leg had been uncomfortable because the boat was rolling and pitching the entire trip. Both Daniela and I were nauseated on and off for most of the journey. Our only glimpse of land had been Isla Margarita way off port side, just a faint outline on the far horizon.

The next land to come into view was the Los Hermanos rocks—the highest one being 600 feet and easily spotted from a distance. The rocks lie 6 miles east of La Blanquilla, which in contrast is a low-lying island, only fifty feet high at its highest point. La Blanquilla is a 72-square-mile limestone island, shaped like an arrowhead. The island is 60 miles north of Juan Griego and 70 miles northwest of Porlamar, Isla Margarita.

Because it is situated on the edge of a deep open trench, La Blanquilla has become the home of Venezuelan wall diving. The wall starts just 65 feet off shore and plummets more than 3,000 feet straight down. The walls are famous for their magnificent, rare black coral, which is becoming increasingly harder to find throughout the world.

We arrived at the bay Playa Falucho, close to the national guard where we had to check in. We made three attempts to anchor but were totally unable to get the anchor to set. We decided to move around to try another bay. The national guard must have been watching us, however, because they came running out onto the shore, jumping up and down and waving their arms in the air, displaying obvious frustration. We tried to call them on the VHF, but that didn't work: they didn't speak English, and unfortunately we didn't speak Spanish, so it was practically impossible to communicate. So Bob and Daniela got in *Whoops-a-Daisy* and went ashore, while I stayed on board and motored *Daisy* around the bay until they returned. This was my first time alone on board while *Daisy* was in motion, and I have to tell you, I was more than a little nervous. The hamster (aka my imagination) was traveling at warp speed on its spinning wheel. I motored nervously around for about twenty minutes. I kept reassuring myself that Captain Bob would never have left me alone if he didn't have complete confidence in my ability to motor *Daisy* safely. This made me question his intelligence. However, all was well. I didn't crash into the mangroves, run aground, or stall the engine, all ideas that the demented hamster had placed carefully in the forefront of my little brain.

After clearing customs, we moved around the island to Playa El Yaque, dropping anchor off what really had to be one of the most delightful beaches in the whole of the Caribbean. The water here truly was crystal clear, deepening off shore to aquamarine before darkening to the deepest blue. The seabed was a mix of sand and coral, and some of the coral heads lay only inches below the surface of the water, so one has to be extremely careful while looking for a safe anchorage. There were four other sailboats anchored off the beach when we arrived.

After lunch, we went ashore to snorkel off the spectacular, pearly pink sandy beach. We saw a magnificent brown spotted trunkfish, some large yellow and blue trumpet fish, a huge colorful parrot fish, along with many different species of butterfly fish, to name just a few. Although what we found to be most amazing was the sheer number of fish; we were literally swimming through shoals of them. They showed little fear and swam happily up to our faces, peering in through our snorkel masks.

Back on the beach, Daniela made friends with a lady called Andi, who was walking her little dog. Andi's boat was anchored alongside ours in the bay; she and her husband were also making their way west toward the Columbian coast.

Later back on board, we sipped cocktails while watching the sunset. After dinner, we all relaxed on deck to stargaze for a while. This island truly is a jewel, a little corner of paradise that only the truly fortunate ever get to experience; access to the island is only by private yacht or small plane. There is a tiny landing strip on the island, but it's used mainly by the coast guard.

Tuesday, August 19

This morning we indulged in a full English breakfast, which we ate on deck while admiring the tropical beauty around us. I'd never seen water like this: turquoise and cerulean, deepening to ultramarine. It was difficult to drag my eyes away. Bob and Daniela went ashore for a hike; meanwhile, I stayed on board to do laundry and cleaning. The national guard told us that they would probably come by in the afternoon, but I never really expected them; they rarely turn up when they say they will.

I sat under the shade of the bimini and repaired our frayed ensign (flag) as best I could. The ensign takes quite a beating between the constant scorching sun and the pounding wind. I didn't know how long the repair would last, but at least the flag was not falling to pieces anymore.

As I expected, both Bob and Daniela got pricked by cactus while hiking. Flowering cactus grow everywhere on the island. They're beautiful to look at, but quick to lose their appeal when they imbed their spines into you. It took us quite a while to remove all the spines from their tender skin.

I made my delicious Fragrant Tuna with Mango and Avocado Salsa for lunch, which we washed down with a lovely, ice-cold, crisp white wine. Bob and I took a rare lazy afternoon nap before venturing ashore in the late afternoon to snorkel again. Danni decided she'd had enough sun for the day, so she stayed on board to rest. On the beach Bob and I ran across Andi and her husband, Roger; we invited them to join us for cocktails later on board *Daisy*. We also met some people from Le Phare Bleu, another couple making their way west to the ABC islands. It's a small world!

The snorkeling here was unbelievable; we saw a multitude of exotic fish, such as a large triggerfish, a French angelfish the size of a dinner plate, colorful butterfly fish, and a group of tiny jewelfish. On the beach I found some gorgeous and unusual shells to add to my steadily growing collection.

After our snorkel, we made another attempt to contact Rene on the SSB, but we were unable to (surprise, surprise). It really was quite frustrating to be out of touch with the outside world.

We were still quite full after our lunch, so I prepared a simple cheese plate for dinner. Bob repaired the fishing pole, and I remade my turtle necklace with fishing line, adding some of the little shells I'd collected on the beach that afternoon. Since living on the boat, I had played around with making jewelry, mostly using the little shells I had collected. The space available on board limited certain hobbies. Fortunately, the beads and shells didn't take up too much room, although Bob always looked nervous when I got out my box of beads: he was always worried about beads falling into and blocking the scuppers (drains) in the cockpit.

Wednesday, August 20

We had more thunder and lightning in the early hours, followed by heavy rain, and we awoke to more rain and heavy cloud cover. Bob said it was simply a wave going through and would pass shortly. By way of a small miracle, we finally managed to make contact on the SSB with Rene at 10 a.m., but there was still no news from either Nicolette or Edward back on the mainland.

Bob fixed the new drop-anchor switch. I topped up the water in the batteries and worked on my journal while we waited for the weather to brighten enough for us to take the dinghy ashore to attach the "doel-fins," which are two wings that attach to the side of the propeller and stop the front of the dinghy from rising out of the water when being driven by only one person. Daniela helped Bob, and I went snorkeling.

Later both Bob and Daniela joined me for a snorkel, but after just a few minutes we noticed the national guard approaching the boats, so we quickly swam back to the dinghy and returned to the boat to wait for them. They visited the new boats that had recently arrived and waved to us as they passed, but they didn't stop to come aboard. We could have stayed and snorkeled longer. Oh well.

After lunch, a Venezuelan fishing boat approached *Daisy*, and we traded a bag of Starbucks coffee for three beautiful red snapper, which I felt was a great deal. The fishermen seemed happy with their exchange, although they originally had requested cigarettes; none of us smoke so we were unable to oblige. When sailing in the western Caribbean, fishing boats often approach sailboats, with the fishermen hoping to trade some of their catch for luxury items like cigarettes. Fishermen will accept almost anything in the way of food or drink. Trading with the fishermen is a great way to get fresh, delicious fish; I find them to have a completely different flavor and texture from the fish one usually buys over the counter.

Daisy at anchor.

We were very busy for the rest of the afternoon getting the boat ready for our sail to Los Roques; Bob expected the leg to take about fifteen hours. Unfortunately, one of the davits broke while bringing *Whoops-a-Daisy* up, and it took a couple of hours to fix.

Our new friends Andi and Roger joined us for a drink at sunset, and Roger helped Bob repair the davits. As Andi, Danni, and I watched the sunset, we clearly saw the "green flash." A green flash is an optical phenomenon that occurs just after sunset or before sunrise. Usually visible for no more than a split second, it may resemble a green ray shooting up from the sunset point just at the second the sun either disappears over the horizon or rises above the horizon. A green flash is usually seen from an unobstructed horizon over an ocean, although it can sometimes be seen from an aircraft or over mountaintops. A sighting is actually quite rare, and many people say there is no such thing. But I can assure you they do exist, having now seen it twice.

After a quick dinner, I got the boat ready for our next leg, and by 9 p.m. we were finally ready to weigh anchor. This was later than we had hoped to leave—the disaster with the davits had set us back a few hours. There was no moon, and we motored slowly out of the bay in total darkness.

Thursday, August 21

Bob took the 9 p.m.-to-midnight watch to get us safely away from the island and reefs. Both Daniela and I rest easier on deck at night when alone on watch; we both feel it's safer to have at least two people in the cockpit in case of emergency. Daniela did the midnight-to-3 a.m. watch, and I did the 3 a.m.-to-6 a.m. watch.

The seas were very calm and there was little to no wind. I felt as though we were in the doldrums, but I wasn't complaining. Lightning storms flashed constantly behind and to starboard of us. I was a little nervous, but fortunately they didn't come too close. The moon that had finally risen cast bright light over the water, so visibility was quite good. The lightning flashed all night, and as day broke, the skies were heavy with cloud cover. The thunder continued to rumble all around us.

Bob took over watch again at 6 a.m., and I went back to bed and slept until 9 a.m. Soon the island of Orchilla was just visible off the port side. We kept our distance, remembering that Orchilla is a military base and boats are not allowed closer than 5 miles. Bob tried to contact Rene on the sideband radio, once again without any luck. Possibly the storms were making connection difficult.

As the first of the islands of Los Roques came into view on the horizon, we still had very heavy cloud cover—not the best way to approach what were supposed to be beautiful islands. Oh well, we hoped to stay for a few days and see the weather brighten up.

We were excited about the prospect of experiencing these fabulous islands for a few days. The Los Roques Archipelago National Park was created in 1972 to protect a marine ecosystem of exceptional natural beauty and ecological value. The area is dominated by coral reefs, mangroves, and sea-grass beds. Los Roques has the reputation of being one of the most beautiful natural areas of Venezuela.

I read that the coral reefs here host some of the most beautiful underwater flora and fauna in the Caribbean. The park boasts exceptionally beautiful beaches of white sand and crystal clear warm water, making it a snorkeling, sailing, and fishing paradise. Los Roques harbors around 60 coral species, 200 crustacean species, 140 mollusk species, 45 echinoderm species, 60 sponge species, along with 280 species of fish. In addition, there are 92 bird species, 50 of which are migratory and can be seen in the park. There are also 4 globally endangered species of sea turtle that nest regularly here.

We motored around to the west side of El Gran Roque, the largest island of the group, and dropped anchor in the bay. After lunch, Bob and Daniela went ashore to visit all the required officials, namely the coast guard, the Inparques, the national guard, and the Los Roques authority, in that order. The officials here are very specific about their check-in instructions. And it's quite expensive as well: they charge $2 per foot for the boat and $12 per person. You are allowed to stay only fifteen days, which can be extended another fifteen days with special permission.

A pelican landed on the bow of the boat, and I got some great pictures before I had to shoo him away (we don't like bird poop on *Daisy*'s deck). Looking over the side, I could see all the way to the ocean bed, which was littered with the most amazing cushion starfish, some the size of dinner plates. When Bob and Daniela returned from customs, we motored around to one of the other islands. Navigating our way through the incredibly shallow water was really difficult and very slow going; I had to stand on the bow to watch for shallow spots or coral just beneath the surface. Meanwhile, I could feel my skin sizzling under the intense sun. The power of the sun's rays out here is really intense; you can burn in a matter of minutes.

After what seemed like hours, we dropped anchor off the beach and were instantly invaded by mosquitoes—swarms of them. We immediately retreated inside, closed all the portholes and hatches, and put on the air-con. I was so grateful for the air-conditioning on *Daisy*: life would have been absolutely unbearable at times without it.

I baked the red snapper for dinner and discovered that there's a real art to filleting a fish—an art that I haven't completely mastered but intend to seriously work on. (See Appendix 3: Preparing Fresh Whole Fish.)

Friday, August 22

I woke early to another beautiful morning. There was a cool breeze blowing, and thankfully there didn't appear to be any mosquitoes, for now at least. (I can but live in hope!) I was covered in so many bites, I looked like I had contracted the measles.

There are thousands, and I do mean thousands, of birds here: gulls, terns, boobies, frigates, and pelicans, to name just a few. They all swarm the fishing boats and form feeding frenzies over the schools of fish in the bay. It's fascinating to watch.

In the late morning, Danni, Bob, and I all got in the dinghy and motored quietly around the bay looking for a place to snorkel. The colors of the water here have to be seen to be believed: Similar to the water around La Blanquilla, the sea changes from the palest cerulean blue, aquamarine, and turquoise then deepens to a dark ultramarine. When I look at the photographs I took of the water around the islands, I still wonder at the incredible array of colors.

We anchored *Whoops-a-Daisy* well off the beach and snorkeled for about half an hour. There wasn't a lot to see other than thousands of jellyfish, so we searched for another spot. We motored slowly around the bay between the islands. We were all so preoccupied, leaning over the side of the dinghy watching the fish and the beautiful coral, that we ran into some rocks. We quickly learned firsthand that the water here between the islands is very shallow, with areas of coral and rock that are deceptive in their distance beneath the surface. Fortunately, we had been driving slowly, so little damage was done to *Whoops-a-Daisy* or the rocks.

We cautiously approached a large area of mangrove trees and through a small archway spotted a beautiful little secluded beach. Bob headed the dinghy carefully through the tunnel of mangroves in the shallow water, attempting to reach the beach. As we passed through the opening in the trees, this time we paid very careful attention to the water, looking for signs of raised coral or rocks under the surface. Consequently, none of us noticed that, as we eased our way through the mangroves, there was a distant, high-pitched buzzing in the air. As we innocently pressed on, we suddenly found ourselves under attack on all sides from millions and millions of mosquitos—swarms of them. It was like a scene from the movie *The Birds*: they were everywhere, all over us. The air was black with them. It was absolutely terrifying.

Trapped in the small confines of the bay with two screaming women and with coral and rocks beneath him, Captain Bob struggled to perform the miraculous 180-degree turn needed to get out of the mangroves at speed.

In desperation, Danni flung herself into the water and, with super-human power, upended the dinghy and dropped it down with the bow now pointing in the right direction. Bob and I stood in the dinghy open mouthed as Danni screamed at us, "Go, go, go!" I grabbed for her as she flung herself back aboard, and Bob gunned the dinghy out through the same opening we had so gingerly picked our way through just a few minutes earlier. We sped out of the opening, trailing what seemed like half the world's population of mosquitoes in our wake. As we were frantically waving our arms, screaming profanities, and crazily beating the insects off each other with towels, two local fishermen watched us with wide-eyed astonishment from their boat and probably found the spectacle highly amusing.

In hindsight, we should have realized that, with that part of the island quite obviously deserted, everyone else already knew what we found out the hard way: that particular island's mangroves are a breeding ground for mosquitoes. The minute we got back to the boat, we showered and covered ourselves with calamine lotion. We were covered in bites everywhere, and I mean everywhere, from head to toe.

I decided that was it: I really didn't like this place. There was absolutely no breeze here, making it easy for the insects to reach the boat, and the heat was suffocating. This was definitely not my idea of paradise: There were crowds of motorboats anchored all along the beach playing loud music; screaming kids being pulled along on doughnuts or water skiing; birds pooping all over our decks; dangerously shallow waters, which are incredibly difficult to navigate; and millions of mosquitoes. I longed to leave.

Danni and I had hoped to leave in the afternoon, but Bob was still in contact with the satellite company, trying to get our system up and working. We were able to pick up a halfway-decent Internet signal here, which we hadn't had since we left Grenada, so he didn't want to move on until it was fixed. We stayed on board for the rest of the day and evening. For dinner I made Grilled Tofu-Sesame Skewers with a Peanut and Ginger Sauce, served with Pearl Couscous with Pomegranate. That was the end of our fresh vegetables. I would have paid almost any price for some fresh fruits or vegetables but needed to manage with what we had on board until we reached Bonaire.

Saturday, August 23

I didn't get much sleep the previous night; the insect bites were driving me insane, my legs were burning and itching like mad. Thank goodness we managed to keep the insects off us at night. The mosquito net we secured over the bed really was a godsend. But as soon as I went out into the galley to make coffee, I got bitten again. I seemed doomed to become a mosquito buffet. Each night I crawled under the mosquito net with arms full of plastic zip bags filled with ice, which I moved from one inflamed area to the next until I was suitably frozen and able to find enough relief to sleep. Then I dreamed of rolling around naked in the snow, only to wake and discover I had rolled over and burst the bag with the melted ice, which explained why I was lying in a pool of freezing water.

In her consistent effort to exercise daily, Daniela swam ashore and back again; the turquoise water was so clear and inviting. A beautiful large box fish was swimming under the boat. We could see it quite clearly, as once again there was no breeze, so the water was perfectly still: it was as if we were looking through glass.

In the afternoon we motored back across the Gran Roques, navigating our way precariously through the shallow waters once again. At times we had less than a foot of water under the boat. As I stood on the bow helping Bob navigate through the passage, the sun was blisteringly hot, and with no breezes to cool us, the temperature was stifling. Once *Daisy* was anchored in the bay, Bob went ashore to check us out. When he returned from customs, we took the dinghy up to the far end of the village.

The little Spanish-style houses were solidly built of stone and brightly painted with pretty inner courtyards filled with brightly flowering plants. I was intrigued by all of the houses' intricately carved wooden doors and shutters that added to the beauty of the little dwellings. The streets here were sand, and there were no cars on the island. The beach was very busy with all the locals return-ing from their day outings and visitors returning from diving trips. All along the beachfront, there were small restaurants with tables spilling out onto the beach, almost reaching to the shore. The atmosphere was one of a relaxed, latent Latin carnival. We stopped in a couple of the local shops and bought some bread and wine, but the supplies were extremely limited.

I cooked breaded shrimp for dinner and served it with coconut rice and tinned sweet corn. It wasn't very special, but I was out of everything fresh. It was all tinned, packet, or frozen food from now on, unless we could catch something.

Sunday, August 24

Bob woke me at the crack of dawn to look at two large fish swimming just off the transom. I wasn't very impressed: I'd been in a deep sleep, having not slept well at all through the night. I would have been much more impressed had he caught the fish, so we would have had something other than frozen food for dinner. He was very excited to see such large fish swimming around the boat, however, so I made the effort to show some enthusiasm.

We had had a lot of rain and quite strong winds in the night; Bob had gotten up a few times throughout the night to check that we were still OK with our holding. After a meager breakfast, we set off for the end of the island chain; this left us just 35 miles from Aves de Barlovento, our next planned stop.

We raised the sails with the hope of sailing without the engine. But with the constantly changing winds, it was too difficult navigating through the shallows, so we brought the sails in and continued under motor. We arrived at one of the far islands, Cayo de Agua, in the early afternoon and dropped anchor exactly as the book instructed, close to the beach in the sandy bottom. We took the dinghy ashore and swam off the beach. A sandy spit joined two tiny uninhabited islands, and the waves crashed spectacularly from either side, creating a magical effect. We were the only boat in the bay: there was nothing around us for miles but water and the two deserted islands. It was absolutely beautiful. The powdery soft, pristinely clean sand without a footprint on it felt like velvet under my feet, and the body-temperature water was like cool silk against my skin. This was certainly closer to my idea of paradise.

Later that evening, after a makeshift dinner, a couple of cocktails, and a bottle of wine, I was just getting ready to go to bed when Bob went up on deck to do his usual nighttime check of the anchor and the dinghy. To his horror, the unthinkable had happened: An unexpected southwesterly wind had picked up and swung *Daisy* 180 degrees. We were stern toward the beach, with only twelve inches of water beneath us, almost aground. I ran up front and brought some chain in to take us farther out, but it made little difference: as the wind and waves continued to build,

Daisy started to ground out. We immediately decided to get the hell out of there while we still could. I brought up the anchor and we set off in total darkness. I was absolutely terrified—my crazy imagination was going into overdrive once again as I thought of every potential disaster that could descend upon us.

Our next planned destination was to have been the Las Aves Archipelago, in particular Aves de Barlovento, which was about five hours away. It was only eleven at night, which meant we could arrive around 4 a.m., when it would still be dark, making it unsafe for us to search for a safe anchorage. We made the decision to keep going all the way to Bonaire. This would make our arrival time in Bonaire around late morning. We couldn't raise the sails due to the abnormal southwesterly winds, so we were forced to continue under motor. The sea was rough, so *Daisy* was rolling around and slamming up and down. After all the cocktails and wine I had consumed that evening, I was, needless to say, quite seasick. I went to bed, leaving Bob to do the night watch alone.

Events such as this leg from Los Roques to Bonaire continued to feed my overactive imagination and kept my fear of sailing alive and kicking. Our near-disaster had left me feeling completely unhinged and, coupled with my seasickness, I was not a happy bunny. I couldn't wait to get to Bonaire and feel some land beneath my feet again.

[Cook's note]

This is a great dish for showcasing wonderful, fresh Caribbean ingredients like tuna, lime, avocado, mango, and ginger. With such a fresh citrus flavor, it will really make your taste buds sit up and take notice.

Fragrant Tuna Steaks with Mango and Avocado Salsa

4 tuna steaks, about 5 to 6 ounces each
Zest of 1 lime
2 tablespoons freshly squeezed lime juice
1 clove garlic, finely diced
1-inch piece fresh ginger, finely grated
2 teaspoons olive oil
½ small jalapeno, seeded and diced
2 teaspoons fennel seeds, toasted
½ teaspoon ground cardamom
1 teaspoon ground cumin
1 teaspoon ground coriander
Pinch of ground star anise
Pinch of sea salt
Freshly ground black pepper
Cilantro, for garnish

1. Remove the skin from the tuna and rinse with water; pat dry with paper towels.
2. In a small bowl combine the lime zest, 1 tablespoon lime juice, garlic, ginger, olive oil, jalapeno, fennel seeds, cardamom, cumin, coriander, star anise, salt, and pepper together to make a paste. Thinly spread the paste on both sides of the steaks.
3. Lightly brush a nonstick grill pan with a little olive oil; place the pan over a high heat. When the pan is hot but not smoking, place the tuna on the grill and press down lightly on the tuna steaks to seal them.
4. Reduce the heat to medium and cook for 5 minutes. Turn the steaks over and cook for an additional 4 to 5 minutes, until cooked to your taste.

Mango and Avocado Salsa:

1 ripe avocado, peeled, pitted, and diced
1 tablespoon lime juice
1 teaspoon fresh ginger juice
1 clove garlic, finely diced
2 medium shallots, finely diced
1 ripe mango, peeled, pitted, and diced
1 tablespoon cilantro, roughly chopped

Mix all ingredients together and serve with the tuna steaks. Make immediately before serving or the avocado will discolor.
Enjoy.

[Cook's note]

Quick, easy, and delicious, this is a great side for when you're in a rush to put something tasty and a little different on a plate. The pomegranate seeds add an interesting texture to the couscous.

Pearl Couscous with Pomegranate

2 cups pearl couscous
4 cups chicken stock
2 star anise
1 large pomegranate
Salt and freshly ground black pepper

1. In a saucepan, prepare the couscous according to the packet directions, substituting chicken stock for water and adding the star anise.
2. Cut the pomegranate in half and carefully remove all the seeds, separating them from the white pith.
3. When the couscous has cooked, remove it from the heat, fluff with a fork, discard the star anise, and season with salt and pepper. Add the pomegranate seeds, stirring to distribute them evenly throughout the couscous.
    Serve warm.
    Enjoy.

[Cook's note]

I discovered a love of Pernod (an anise-flavored liqueur) during my years traveling in the South of France, where it's widely used in many fish dishes. I especially love the flavor of Pernod with red snapper.

Red Snapper Braised with Pernod and Fennel

3 tablespoons olive oil
1 yellow onion, sliced
2 stalks celery, sliced
2 medium carrots, peeled, halved, and sliced
1 medium fennel bulb, sliced
4 cloves garlic, minced
2 tablespoons fresh dill, chopped, plus sprigs for garnish
½ teaspoon Maldon sea salt flakes
Freshly ground pepper
2 whole red snappers, about 2 to 3 pounds each
½ cup Pernod
½ cup fish stock

1. Preheat the oven to 400 degrees F.
2. Heat the oil in a large sauté pan over medium-high heat. Add the onion, celery, carrot, fennel, and garlic; sauté until soft, about 5 minutes. Stir in the dill; add salt flakes and pepper to taste. Transfer two-thirds of the vegetable mixture to an ovenproof baking dish large enough to lay the fish flat.
3. Cut 4 angled slits on each side of the fish, about halfway to the bone. Place the fish on top of the vegetables, scatter the remaining vegetables over the fish.
4. Place the sauté pan back over medium heat, and add the Pernod and fish stock. Bring to a gentle simmer and deglaze the pan, scraping up any browned bits from the pan bottom. Simmer for 1 minute; pour over the fish and vegetables.
5. Cover the baking dish with foil. Bake for about 30 minutes, basting occasionally with the pan juices until the fish is opaque throughout. Test the doneness by inserting an instant-read thermometer into the thickest part of the fish; it will be ready when the thermometer registers 140 degrees F. Remove from the oven and serve on a warm platter, garnished with dill sprigs. Enjoy.

Grilled Tofu-Sesame Skewers with a Peanut and Ginger Sauce

½ cup freshly squeezed orange juice
4 tablespoons lite soy sauce, divided
1 tablespoon toasted sesame oil
3 cloves (about 2 teaspoons) garlic, minced, divided
1 fresh red chili pepper, seeds removed, finely diced
1 (12-ounce) packet extra-firm smoked tofu, cut into 1-inch cubes *(see note below)*
¼ cup organic creamy peanut butter
3 tablespoons fresh ginger, peeled and finely chopped
2 tablespoons light brown sugar

1. Combine the orange juice, 2 tablespoons soy sauce, sesame oil, 1 teaspoon garlic, and chili pepper. Pour the mixture into a plastic zip bag. Add the tofu and marinate for at least 1 hour, or overnight, stirring occasionally.
2. Preheat a grill or an oven broiler. If using a broiler, coat the broiler pan with cooking spray.
3. Thread the tofu on wooden skewers. If you're using a broiler pan, place the skewers on the broiler pan. Broil or grill 5 to 7 minutes or until lightly browned on all sides, turning occasionally. *(Note: Soak the wooden skewers in cold water for 1 hour before using.)*
4. **To make the sauce:** Whisk together the peanut butter, remaining 1 teaspoon garlic, ginger, brown sugar, remaining soy sauce, and ⅓ cup warm water to make a thick sauce.
   Serve skewers with dipping sauce.
   Enjoy.

(Note: Here's the best way to drain excess liquid from tofu: Remove the tofu from the pack, draining off all the water. Wrap it thickly in sheets of kitchen paper towels and place it in a dish with a weight on the top to press all the liquid out of the tofu. Set it aside at room temperature for at least 1 hour. Change the kitchen paper towels frequently until all of the liquid has drained out and the tofu feels dry.)

Nic, fun on the phone, St. Barts

Afternoon nap

Bob and Nicho-San relaxing in the air-chair.

Edi with a Trunk fish skeleton.

Taking a nap while Mum's on watch

Snorkeling in the clear Caribbean water

The long wade to ashore

Danni 'time out' in a beach hammock

Chapter 13

Los Roques to Bonaire

Coordinates: Bonaire 12 10'N 68 14'W

Monday, August 25

E n route to Bonaire. The effects of the previous night's wine and cocktail combination had taken its toll on me, and despite the rather rough conditions, I managed a few hours' sleep. Bob woke me at 6 a.m. to take the morning watch while he grabbed a few well-deserved hours of sleep. Storm clouds lay heavily behind us, but fortunately the direction in which we were headed looked promising. I could just glimpse the Isla de Aves on the horizon. Barlovento and Sotavento are two archipelagos separated by about 10 miles of deep water. They got their names from the large number of birds that make the islands their home. The larger of the islands has dense mangrove forests. There wasn't a chance in a million that I was going anywhere near those areas, after my experience in Los Roques with the mosquitoes.

The water was quite calm as we motored along, but we still had the south-westerly wind making it impossible for us to sail. We were, however, making a steady 8 knots. A school of bottlenose dolphins swam alongside and behind the boat; one of them leaped out of the water right alongside the helm where I was standing. I will never cease to be thrilled each time I see these magnificent creatures in their natural environment.

We found a flying fish on the deck. It was dead obviously, so Daniela and I had the bright idea of using it as bait. We put the fishing line out, and after about an hour we managed to haul in a beautiful tuna. "Yeah!" we both exclaimed excitedly. "Sushi for dinner!" We had to haul the tuna aboard quickly before the gathering flock of frigate birds circling the boat above us swooped down to steal it.

We were quick to kill the tuna by pouring vodka into its gills, and then we packed it in ice to keep it fresh. All tuna quickly deteriorates, especially once cut into steak portions, so I knew we had to refrigerate it immediately, preferably whole, or cover it with crushed ice and try to use it within one day. This tuna wasn't going to last that long: the idea of fresh fish for lunch and dinner was just too exciting.

A comical group of three flamingos flew past, and I couldn't help but wonder where they were headed so far from land. They always appear to be in such a panic when they fly; it's as if they're about to crash at any moment. They're really quite hysterically funny to watch.

As the sun came up and the heat intensified, I fixed a blanket up behind the helm to shield us. By 8 a.m. Bonaire appeared through a misty haze on the horizon. Approaching from the east, the high land of the island in the north is the first to become visible. The southern part of the island barely peeps above sea level. The ocean is thousands of feet deep all around the island, rising suddenly to only a few hundred feet close to shore, and then shallowing tremendously to only twenty feet very quickly. If it were possible to observe the island underwater from a distance, you would see that it's shaped like a mushroom, with all the land above water level appearing to stand on a pillar.

We motored around the west coast of the island to Kralendijk, the capital of Bonaire, where we picked up a mooring. No anchoring is allowed anywhere around Bonaire; the entire island is a marine park. We headed ashore to visit customs and immigration. The coastline of Bonaire is absolutely beautiful—a rainbow of colors, brightly painted modern condos and houses, and beachfront restaurants and bars bustling with people. Palm trees and colorful plants line the roadside along the coast. On first inspection, the island appears very cosmopolitan and modern, really well cared for, unlike many of the other Caribbean islands.

After customs and immigration, we walked around the town of Kralendijk, then sat and had a cocktail on the pier before returning to *Daisy* for dinner. At dusk the mosquitoes swarmed the boat, so we had to shut up quickly and put on the air-con. We spent a quiet evening relaxing inside watching television.

Tuesday, August 26

In the morning I had the delightful job of cleaning out the fridge. In our haste to get away from Los Roques in the night, a bowl of soup that I had carelessly placed in the fridge had upturned, creating a horrible mess. This did provide me with a good excuse to clean and sterilize and be ready for reprovisioning later. Late morning we took *Whoops-a-Daisy* across to the marina so Bob could check on the slip he'd booked. Unfortunately, we found the marina office closed. We were unaware that most businesses were shut here between noon and 2 p.m., so we took the dinghy across to the other side of the marina and sat in La Balandra restaurant overlooking the ocean. There were a few iguanas moving around between the tables. Both Danni and Bob scowled at me when they caught me sneaking food under the table for them. I refrained from my iguana feeding, and we ordered margaritas and shared a large dish of nachos. After lunch we returned to the office, only to discover that no slip had been reserved for us. The marina manager, who had made our reservation six weeks before, was apparently away on vacation, and the office could find no details of our booking, despite having taken our credit card information over the phone. They promised to find room for us and said we could move into a slip on Friday; they could squeeze us in between two other boats, they said. I find docking hard enough when we have a slip all to ourselves; squeezing in between two other boats was going to be a real challenge. We could always hope for a windless day. "Oh well," I thought. "This could be another chapter for my journal."

Later that afternoon, we took *Whoops-a-Daisy* over to the airport to arrange a rental car for the next day. Once the car was organized, we went into town and walked around to do some sightseeing. It didn't take long: the island capital was really quite small. We arrived at the Mona Lisa, reputed to be the best restaurant in Kralendijk. Luckily, they had a table for us and we had a really lovely meal, with the restaurant more than living up to its great reputation. Daniela was in high spirits, the food was good, and we were all having a very fun evening.

That night, after a couple of hours of failed attempts at sleep, Bob and I got up to check outside. The boat was rolling quite violently, and poor old *Whoop-a-Daisy*, which was unusually left down, was now crashing and banging in protest against the stern. Unfortunately, the wind had once again switched to a southwesterly, and we were stern in to the seawall. The boat alongside us had also swung 180 degrees on its mooring and was swinging dangerously close to Daisy. We watched for a while as the lightning flashed spectacularly all around us, the waves built, and *Whoops-a-Daisy* continued to bounce and crash about on the stern.

Bob decided to bring the dingy up on the davits before it got damaged. I ran around frantically putting fenders out to protect us from bumping into our neighbor, while Daniela tried to help Bob with the dinghy. It was quite a difficult operation. Poor Bob tried to maintain his balance as the dinghy bounced wildly about and he struggled to attach the davits. To my immense relief, they eventually succeeded and brought the dinghy up safely without incident. Daniela returned to bed, but Bob and I stayed up on watch for a while. When we finally returned to bed, I found that I still couldn't sleep; the boat was still rocking and rolling violently and pulling hard on her mooring lines; my vivid imagination was once again working overtime, dreaming up every possible disaster waiting to befall us.

Wednesday, August 27

Hooray, we survived the night intact with no damage done, other than my being exhausted from a totally sleepless night. That'll teach me not to have more confidence in Captain Bob's decisions regarding *Daisy*.

The car we had rented was due to be delivered to the pier at 9:30 a.m. We sat and waited for an hour, and it eventually arrived at 10:30 a.m. This type of service is not unusual in the islands. We should have been quite used to it by now, but it never failed to frustrate Bob. I often wondered whether he would ever accept "island time." Everyone in the Caribbean is so laid-back; they're never in a rush to do anything. Don't ever expect anything to happen quickly or on time, or you'll live with permanent disappointment!

After completing the paperwork, we went to the local supermarket to do some provisioning then took the groceries back to the boat. It was such a relief to finally have some fresh fruit and vegetables again. I often wonder how people who spend months at sea manage. They must live on rice, potatoes, and pasta. Unfortunately, Captain Bob doesn't eat starchy carbs, so that's not an option for us, and after a few days at sea our supply of fresh fruit and vegetables is usually all gone. The only produce that keeps fresh for longer than a few days are potatoes, onions, and butternut squash. (See Appendix 2: Galley Notes.)

We had a quick bite to eat before returning to the island to set off on our tour of discovery. As we drove around the island, we saw flamingos, wild donkeys, and a lot of the island's small but beautiful little bright green and yellow parrots called prikichi. Like all parrots, they were quite noisy.

The island is very dry and desertlike, covered with many different kinds of cactus and scrub. Bonaire is reputed to have some of the world's best dive sites, and we saw divers at every bay we stopped at. We drove on up to the national park, but the gate attendant said we were too late in the day to complete even the short tour of the park. So we drove on around the island and stopped at a large lagoon with one of the island's popular windsurfing beaches. It was much too crowded for my liking, and I wasn't very impressed. I guess I've been thoroughly spoiled with all the beautiful deserted beaches that I've become accustomed to.

We ordered margaritas at the bar, but the bartenders seemed to have difficulty understanding that Daniela wanted a frozen one and I wanted one on the rocks. Eventually, after much ado, they appeared to sort it out, but then they proceeded to serve us the most disgusting, undrinkable, dreadful excuse for margaritas that we've ever had. Mine tasted like warm dishwater. Daniela immediately returned hers and asked for a beer: She told them quite openly that it was nasty. I simply left mine on the table and determined never to return to that beach or particularly to that dreadful bar again.

We drove back to the boat, and Bob helped me prepare dinner and clean up, because I was feeling quite tired. I went to bed right after dinner and quickly fell into a deep sleep.

Friday, August 29

I woke very early, before Bob or Danni, and eagerly grabbed the opportunity to work on my journal. Creeping quietly up on deck with my trusty Mac tucked under my arm, I was just in time to see the rising sun. The bay was peaceful and still, like a painting. The sun's brilliant rays pierced through the scattered clouds and cast paths of blinding gold and crimson light across the water.

I hoped that we could move the boat into the marina that day. I wanted to get her settled before both Bob and Daniela had to leave on Friday. The morning's chores involved cleaning the mess off the side of the boat that had been left by the storm. The water in the bay was lovely to swim in, but one wouldn't really want to get in the water at the marina, so the cleaning needed to be done prior to us going alongside. Midmorning we moved the boat around to the fuel dock and filled the diesel tanks. Bob went into the office to find out which slip we were booked into, only to discover that they had forgotten we were coming in, despite the fuss we made four days ago about their losing our reservation and their assurances that they would find another slip for us. It turned out they had given our reserved slip to another yacht that had arrived two days before. So Bob made yet more arrangements for us to take the boat in the next day at 9 a.m., just before his scheduled departure. At that point, I was really praying that they would find a slip for *Daisy*; otherwise, I would be looking at three weeks out on the mooring, and I really didn't want that, given our previous experience with the shifting winds here. We took *Daisy* back onto the mooring for the night and went ashore for dinner at La Balandra, the harbor restaurant at the resort.

Saturday, August 30

Bob got up at 5 a.m. to drive Daniela to the airport for her 7 a.m. flight home. When he returned, we moved the boat around to the marina. Surprise, surprise, they weren't ready for us, but it didn't take them long to find us a slip. Having finally got the boat situated, Bob packed his bags and grabbed a quick lunch before the taxi picked him up to take him to the airport.

The marina had another surprise for me: There was no Internet, despite their advertisement that said they had Wi-Fi. (There was also no laundry on-site, as advertised.) I determined that trekking to the Internet cafe, which was a five-minute walk up the road, would have to do for now. There was a beautiful beach, and the marina was quiet and safe. I made the decision to relax and do some painting.

Sunday, August 31, through Friday, September 5

Alone on the boat in Kralendijk harbor marina, Bonaire, I spent my days painting, snorkeling, lying on the beach—generally relaxing and being lazy. Oh, what a lovely change. Although the weather was extraordinarily hot and at times unbearable. I sweated all the time; it was quite disgusting. Having lived in the islands for a year, I thought I would be used to the heat by now, but this was intense. I walked to the Internet cafe every day until I managed to find a contact in town that sold me an Internet connection for the boat.

Saturday, September 6

On Bonaire Day, biker enthusiasts arrive in huge numbers from Curacao and Aruba, shipping their bikes over for this special weekend. Harleys, Ducatis, Triumphs, every possible bike you can imagine, invaded the island. Then they all circumnavigated the island in a convoy. It was quite spectacular to watch, but I really needed ear plugs: it was deafening to listen to, and there was nowhere to escape the noise. The entire island rumbled all day long with the vibrations from all the engines.

I woke at 3 a.m., too excited to sleep any longer: Niki was due to arrive at 5 a.m. I left the boat at 4:25 a.m. to drive to the airport. Nicolette's plane landed shortly after 5 a.m., but it took over an hour to clear everyone through customs. Niki and I arrived back at the boat at 6:15 a.m. I made her some scrambled eggs, then she crawled into bed for a few hour's sleep.

After lunch Niki and I went across to the local beach to snorkel. Nicolette was as amazed by the marine life as I had been on my first snorkel trip here. The reefs around Bonaire boast spectacular gardens of coral, underwater flora, crustaceans, and some really colorful and unusual varieties of sponges. We saw some of the largest stovepipe sponges that I've ever seen, along with hundreds of feather duster worms (or fan worms). It was really hard to tear ourselves away, but Bob was due back from his trip and I didn't want to be away from *Daisy* when he arrived. Niki and I got back to the boat just as the taxi was dropping Bob off. As soon as he was unpacked and changed, we grabbed a bite to eat and relaxed with a cocktail for a few minutes on deck before returning to the beach for another snorkel. I just couldn't stay out of the water. As a snorkeling and diving destination, this island was hard to beat. Of all the islands I've visited, Bonaire was far and away the best for this sport.

For dinner I made a succulent spicy chicken satay with stir-fried vegetables. And after dinner we sat up on deck playing Mexican Train, sipping cocktails under the star-filled sky.

Sunday, September 7

In the morning we moved *Daisy* out of the marina and put her back on a mooring in the bay. The Bonaire bike weekend continued. With hundreds of bikes all over the island, it was incredibly noisy but, fortunately, it was a little less noisy out on the mooring. After lunch, Niki, Bob, and I snorkeled off the boat. This was a first for me: I've always been so frightened of deep water that I've never had the courage to swim more than a few feet from the boat, and even then I used one of those floaty noodle things, the sort that four-year-olds use. Yes, I was that pathetic, but fortunately times have changed. This time I swam to the shore, snorkeled for a while, then swam back to the boat. I seemed to have conquered my fear of swimming in deep water, and for the first time I could honestly say that I wasn't nervous. I would even go so far as to say that I enjoyed it. The marine life around Bonaire was just too tempting to miss, and

I wasn't about to let my fear of deep water prevent me from enjoying possibly some of the best snorkeling I would ever get to experience. It took a lot of courage for me to do it: it was a huge step forward but, having done it, I've never looked back.

Unfortunately, I enjoyed the snorkeling a little too much. I had spent so much time in the water that my back was burnt to a crisp, red like a lobster fresh from the pot. It's very easy to forget how strong the sun is out here, especially when you're in the water. When I made hot chicken curry for dinner that night, Niki joked about my being hot inside and out. Between the sunburn and the red-hot curry, I really was burning up! Not perhaps the best choice for dinner under the circumstances. After dinner and a couple of cocktails, we watched the movie *Harry Potter and the Order of the Phoenix*. True to form, I fell asleep in the middle of the movie—the sun and snorkeling had really worn me out.

Monday, September 8

After an early rise and a light breakfast, Bob and Niki set about cleaning and polishing the stainless fittings on the boat, while I did the dishes and cleaned up inside. By late morning we finished our chores and headed into town to shop and look for a new snorkeling mask for Bob. We stopped for lunch at the City Café on the seafront before walking to the supermarket to do some grocery shopping. After we had unloaded our purchases back at the boat, we took *Whoops-a-Daisy* around to the Andreas II dive site. The Andreas is a shipwreck just off the Bonaire coast. It's a very popular spot for divers and has several markers for both snorkelers and divers. We tied up to a buoy and snorkeled off the dinghy, which was another first for me. Confession time: If truth be told, it wasn't only the fear of deep water that prevented me all these years from swimming off the dinghy. The fact is, at some point I would have to get back *into* the dinghy, which is not a graceful exercise at the best of times, particularly for yours truly. I knew everyone would have to get in the dinghy before me, and then they would all have to heave-ho and haul me out of the water and up over the side like a beached whale. So, in order to avoid this humiliating experience, it was easier to simply not get in the water in the first place. But the beautiful waters of Bonaire could not be missed, so I was determined to deal with the humiliation when the time came. As it turned out I was right, and once again the Bonaire marine life proved itself well worthy of any humiliation that I had to suffer in order to enjoy it.

The water was so clear and the seabed spectacular, like a colorful garden with an amazing array of anemones and coral life, hundreds of different species of fish and, best of all, a curious young turtle that was not much bigger than a dinner plate and was not at all shy. We swam with him for a while, and I took some fabulous photographs. As the turtle swam close to the surface, the beautiful patterns of his green and gold shell shimmered in the sunlit water.

The Andreas II is a novice dive site with only slight currents. It's reachable from boat or shore. The maximum depth is thirty meters (ninety-eight feet), and average visibility is twenty meters (sixty-five feet). We read that, if you're lucky, you may spot sea horses here. Some people on the island had told us of a few recent sightings, although we didn't manage to see any. This is a shame because sighting sea horses would more than have made up for the hilarious and humiliating spectacle of my clumsy attempts at hauling my lardy ass back into the dinghy after the snorkel.

Sufficiently recovered from the day's events, I enjoyed cocktails at the pier bar with Bob and Niki and dinner at one of the seafront restaurants. We returned to *Daisy* to watch *Harry Potter* again, and this time I managed to watch the whole movie without falling asleep.

[Cook's note]

I am an avid cheese lover, and this recipe is one of my favorites, especially for a light lunch. It's quick, easy, and thoroughly delicious, absolutely wonderful served with a good red wine. Because of the heat and humidity in the Caribbean, it's best to leave the Brie and the pastry in the refrigerator until the last minute. The first time I made this on board I had set out all my ingredients thirty minutes before I was ready to start, so when I tried to cut the Brie it had turned to liquid, and the pastry had completely stuck to the board. I never made that mistake again.

Brie Baked in Pastry

1 tablespoon walnuts, toasted and chopped
1 (8-ounce) round Brie cheese
1 tablespoon apricot jam
1 tablespoon dried apricots, chopped
1 small sprig fresh rosemary leaves, finely chopped
1 tablespoon dried unsweetened cranberries
1 sheet puff pastry (either store-bought or homemade)
1 egg, lightly beaten

1. Preheat the oven to 400 degrees F.
2. Toast the walnuts in a dry nonstick pan over a medium heat for 2 to 3 minutes. Shake the pan to move the walnuts around while toasting; be careful not to let them burn. Set aside.
3. Cut the Brie round horizontally into two halves.
4. In a small saucepan, warm the apricot jam over low heat. Do not boil.
5. Mix the apricots, rosemary leaves, walnuts, and cranberries into the jam. Let it cool, then spread the mixture over the cut surfaces and reassemble the cheese rounds.
6. Cut two circles of puff pastry, each about ¾ inch larger than the Brie.
7. Place one of the pastry rounds on a parchment-lined or greased cooking tray. Place the cheese in the center of the round. Bring the pastry up the sides, and press the cheese to make smooth and even.

8. In a small bowl, lightly whisk the egg with 2 tablespoons water. Set aside.
9. Cover the cheese with the second round. Brush edges with the egg wash, and smooth over the round to completely encase the Brie.
10. Bake for 20 minutes or until the pastry is golden brown.
    Serve with apple wedges, grapes, and fresh-baked baguette slices.
    Enjoy.

[Cook's note]

This is one of Nicolette's favorite dishes, but she likes it best when it's served cold. Her friend Sam said it was the best couscous he has ever eaten, so I thought I should include it here. This is a fairly easy and uncomplicated method, and it keeps for days in the fridge. Although there are a lot of ingredients, you can basically add any vegetables you want—it's consistently good. I sometimes eat this as a meal by itself, but it also perfectly complements fish.

Winter Vegetable Couscous

¾ cup split peas
4½ cups chicken or vegetable stock, divided
1 cup pearl couscous
4 tablespoons unsalted butter
1 medium red onion, diced small
2 medium carrots, peeled and diced small
1 zucchini, diced small
8 ounces assorted mushrooms, cleaned and sliced
1 yellow bell pepper, seeded and diced
½ yellow jalapeno pepper, seeded and finely diced
1 level teaspoon cumin
¼ cup sun-dried tomatoes, sliced (I like the sun-dried tomatoes in oil, but dried will also work)
½ cup pine nuts, toasted
1 tablespoon soy sauce
Salt and black pepper

1. Put 2½ cups of stock in a large saucepan over high heat and bring it to a boil. Add the split peas, reduce heat to low, cover, and simmer for 30 minutes. Drain and set aside.
2. In a separate medium-size saucepan, stir in the couscous, the remaining 2 cups of stock, and 2 tablespoons of the butter. Bring to a boil, reduce heat to low, cover, and simmer for 10 minutes. When all the liquid is absorbed, remove from the heat and set aside.

3. In a large sauté pan over medium heat, add the rest of the butter. When the butter starts sizzling, add the onions and cook gently, stirring occasionally until translucent but not brown.
4. To the onions add the carrots, zucchini, mushrooms, bell pepper, jalapeno, and cumin. Sauté about 3 or 4 minutes, or until the vegetables are soft.
6. To the vegetables add the sun-dried tomatoes, pine nuts, soy sauce, split peas, and couscous; season to taste with salt and pepper.
   Serve hot or cold.
   Enjoy.

Chicken and Cashews with Cilantro

1½ pounds boneless, skinless chicken thighs, cut into 1-inch cubes
8 ounces assorted mushrooms, cleaned and sliced
2 tablespoons peanut oil
6 ounces fresh green beans, trimmed and halved
2 medium carrots, thinly sliced
½ cup cashew halves, toasted
½ cup cilantro, roughly chopped
For the marinade:
2 tablespoons peanut oil
1 teaspoon toasted sesame oil
2 teaspoons cumin seeds, toasted
1 tablespoon mirin or Japanese rice wine
2 cloves garlic, chopped
1 tablespoon fresh ginger, grated
Grated zest and juice of 2 limes
Salt and pepper to taste

1. In a small bowl, mix together the ingredients for the marinade, season with salt and pepper, and pour into a plastic zip bag. Add the chicken cubes to the marinade and mix well. Let it marinate in the refrigerator for 1 hour. Drain, reserving the marinade. Set aside.
2. Heat a wok until hot. Add the oils, then toss in half the chicken and stir-fry until golden brown, about 3 to 4 minutes. Remove the chicken with a slotted spoon, drain on kitchen paper towels, and keep warm. Repeat with the remaining chicken.
3. Put the mushrooms, green beans, and carrots in the wok and stir-fry for another 2 to 3 minutes. Add the cashews. Pour in the remaining marinade, then add the chicken and heat thoroughly over medium heat. Add a splash of water if the mixture becomes too dry.
Sprinkle with the chopped cilantro leaves and serve.
Enjoy.

[Cook's note]

This recipe takes me back to my childhood in Bristol, England: My nan used to make the most delicious melt-in-the-mouth shortbread. I added some pumpkin pie spice to her recipe as an experiment; it's a departure from the traditional shortbread but still delicious.

Pumpkin Pie Spiced Shortbread

6 large free-range egg yolks
½ cup soft brown sugar
8 tablespoons salted butter, softened
1¼ cups all-purpose flour
1 teaspoon pumpkin pie spice
1½ teaspoons baking powder

1. Using either a food mixer or large bowl and a hand mixer, beat the eggs yolks and sugar together until thick and creamy; slowly beat in the softened butter. Sift in the flour, pumpkin pie spice, and baking powder. Mix ingredients together, then knead to form a soft dough.
2. Wrap the dough in plastic wrap and refrigerate for 30 minutes.
3. Preheat the oven to 300 degrees F.
4. Remove the dough from the fridge, and, on a floured surface, gently form it into a ball. Roll the dough out to about a ¾-inch thickness and place it on a nonstick baking tray. Using a sharp knife, score the top into segments, being careful not to cut all the way through.
5. Bake for about 20 to 25 minutes until the top is golden brown. Enjoy.

Chapter 14

Bonaire to Aves de Sotavento

Coordinates: Sotavento 12 10'00"N 67 34'00"W

Thursday, September 11

Still on a mooring in a Bonaire bay. Bob went ashore at 8 a.m. to clear customs and immigration, and we set sail as soon as he returned. We had a reasonable crossing but no good wind, so we were unable to set the sails. We arrived at Aves de Sotavento in the early evening and dropped anchor alongside one of the islands, which are all very tiny and extremely remote. There are mature mangroves and scrub, but not much more in the way of vegetation. And there are no inhabitants other than a small coast guard station and a handful of fishermen who live here for about three months each year. The tiny islands are covered with mounds and mounds of conch shells left by fishermen. The conch are removed from the shells and stored in iceboxes on the fishing boats to transport back to the mainland for sale; the empty shells are then discarded on the islands.

Las Aves Archipelago is comprised of two reefs known as the Windward and Leeward Aves. They are located between Los Roques to the east and Bonaire to the west. The name Las Aves ("the birds") derives from the numerous birds that live in or migrate to the bird sanctuary there. The Aves are also famous for shipwrecks: one of the most frequently told stories tells of a fleet of fifteen French warships that were intercepted by the Dutch on their way to attack Curacao in 1678.

I tried to find out as much as I could about these islands before we started our trip, but not much has been written about them, so I relied mainly on blogs written by previous visitors.

Nic and camera

Friday, September 12

Just after breakfast the coast guard arrived, a group of five polite young men. It was really difficult communicating with them: they didn't speak any English, and as you may remember from our previous fiascos with island coast guards, we speak no Spanish. Although with much patience, perseverance, trial and error, and a lot of sign language and pointing, we eventually managed to complete the paperwork. It was quite an exhausting exercise. The coastguardsmen were all extremely helpful and very friendly. In fact, they seemed quite comfortable on board *Daisy* and, because we were the only boat in the vicinity, in no apparent hurry to leave. They were keen to see inside *Daisy*, and Bob graciously gave them a tour. I served them all soft drinks and began to get the feeling they were making themselves comfortable for the day.

Eventually they did return to their post, and we prepared to go snorkeling. We took the dinghy across to the island and set the anchor so we could swim from the dinghy. My newfound bravado in the water was not required around the islands of the Aves, because the water was so shallow. The snorkeling was good—we saw some lovely species of parrot fish, damsels, and trunkfish—but nothing quite as spectacular as the reef life off the shores of Bonaire. The sun was incredibly intense. It's very easy to forget how dangerous the sun is when you're swimming; the water keeps your body cool, and you're often not aware of the damage done until you get out of the water.

We returned to the boat for cocktails, Chicken Waldorf Salad, and blue cheese coleslaw with dried cranberries. After dinner we played Mexican Train. Fortunately, Nicolette seemed to enjoy the game as much as I did.

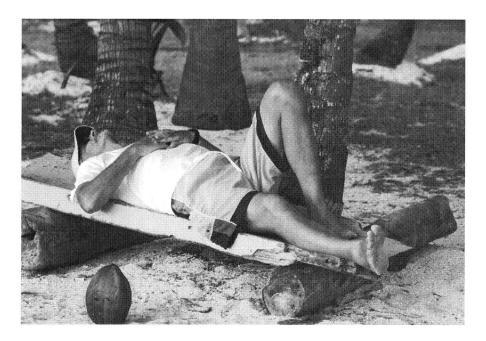

A rare sight, Captain Bob relaxing!

Saturday, September 13

Niki was nursing a painful sunburn and decided to stay in the shade. We spent a relaxing day on board: I painted, Niki sketched and read a book, and Bob repaired the broken icemaker. In the late afternoon, Bob and I went for another snorkel, but my face was sore from too much sun and the waves were rough, so we returned after only a short time. In the early evening when the sun wasn't so strong, we attempted to go back to the island with Niki. But we were unable to anchor the dinghy because the waves had become very rough, so we returned to *Daisy*. After dinner we watched another movie (one of my favorites, *Tomb Raider*) and, as usual, I fell asleep halfway through. All the clean fresh air and swimming had really exhausted me, although I have to add that whenever I'm on board I always fall asleep early. I tend to rise with the sun and go to bed with it. It's the way of a sailor!

Sunday, September 14

We left Aves de Sotavento in the early morning and had a very sunny but rolly, uncomfortable sail across to Bonaire. We arrived at 2 p.m. and picked up a mooring on the front. Bob and Niki left to pay for the mooring and then go snorkeling. I didn't feel like snorkeling, so I stayed on board and did laundry instead. Why is it that I always seem to have so much more laundry on the boat than I do in a house?

Niki lost one of her brand-new TUSA flippers at the Andreas II dive site. And following a long search of the site, Bob and Niki were unable to find it, so needless to say, the flipper added some extra color to the coral reefs and probably became home for a local fish.

Monday, September 15

Early in the morning we called Edi at his school, the College of Creative Studies in Detroit, to wish him a happy twenty-fifth birthday. Then we spent the rest of the morning getting the boat ready for sail. We weighed anchor at 11 a.m., slightly later than we had hoped to leave, but were still due to arrive in Curacao well before nightfall. With smooth, calm seas and a good wind, 18 to 25 knots for the entire leg, the sail down the side of Bonaire was lovely. But once we cleared the island, the seas became much choppier, and we averaged a steady 8 knots. As we approached Curacao in the late afternoon, the waves became larger and the wind much stronger. It had been quite a rough sail for about thirty minutes until we cleared around the island.

We started our approach through the entrance to Spanish Waters. When coming in here, it's advisable to stay close to the beach, which is still ninety feet deep. You can easily see the shallow reef edge to the north then zigzag your way through the channel. This is not a place you would want to navigate in the dark: the entrance is not lit or marked with buoys, so you need to arrive in good light. We approached with extreme caution. Spanish Waters is a landlocked lagoon surrounded by beautiful houses. We dropped anchor in one of the bays among a lot of other sailboats.

My first impression of Curacao was surprisingly pleasant. I had been reluctant to visit the island because of its reputation for high crime rates, drugs, and general lack of security. What's more, Curacao was known as a center for pirates in the eighteenth century, and rumor had it not much had changed. That's why, upon our approach, I was amazed at the grand villas and houses that lined the entrance and surrounded the harbor. The Curacao Yacht Club looked very swish and expensive (but apparently is for members only). The craggy cliff faces that towered over both sides of the harbor looked almost prehistoric. Other than the cliffs, the land appeared very flat. The abundance of cactus told me this is a very dry island. So far Curacao looked beautiful, but further exploration would reveal the truth.

I made Portobello Mushrooms with Mascarpone, Blue Cheese, and Basil with Moroccan Couscous for dinner, and Niki put on everybody's favorite movie, *Pirates of the Caribbean*, which somehow seemed quite fitting given our location at that time!

Tuesday, September 16

I got up early again to write in my journal; a quiet hour spent writing before breakfast enabled me to write all my blog notes before I got involved with the plans for the day ahead. I started blogging shortly after beginning my life aboard, mainly so that my family could follow my adventures. I wrote daily in my journal when circumstances allowed and published my stories and photos on the blog when we were able to pick up Internet access.

Bob had arranged for a rental car to be delivered to the pier so we could explore the island. The island had the reputation of being the ugly industrial sister of beautiful Bonaire, so I was eager to discover for myself if this were true. From my research, the difference is Curacao has the infrastructure that's missing from most of the southeastern Caribbean islands. In fact, Curacao is rated as second in the world for snorkeling, even above Bonaire, thanks to its white coral sand beaches and crystal clear water. So I intended to ignore all the negative comments I'd heard and read about this island and explore it as if I'd heard nothing.

Our first stop was Willemstad, where we parked the car on the seafront and wandered past colorful tourist stalls selling everything from handmade jewelry, pottery, and paintings to small items of furniture, fabrics, and knickknacks.

Designated a UNESCO World Heritage site in 1977, Willemstad is the capital of Curacao. Its older area is made up of distinct districts, with architectural styles reflecting the seventeenth century Dutch colonization of the ABC islands. The Sint Annabaai is a channel linking the sea to the inner harbor. It divides the central city into Otrobanda, a primarily residential area, and Punda, the commercial area. One of the major landmarks in Willemstad is the floating pontoon bridge named the Queen Emma; it spans the channel and swings open to allow passage for ships.

The Queen Emma Bridge swings back and forth continuously throughout the day to let people cross and boats pass through. When the bridge is closed, a ferry shuttles passengers back and forth, and it's always full.

The Queen Emma bridge

I was amazed by the number of people who constantly crossed from one side to another. We stopped at one of the waterside cafes and drank cups of really strong coffee while we watched the people and the boats. After all the caffeine, I would be bouncing off the walls later. A local man carrying two large pet iguanas on his shoulders paraded up and down along the cafes, stopping occasionally to chat with the tourists. I thought it rather sad and ironic that one of the shorefront restaurants listed iguana meat on its menu.

We waited for the floating bridge to reopen then walked across to find the immigration office. It was quite a long, uncomfortable walk in the intense heat. We arrived at the offices hot and sweaty, and then had to sit and wait in the freezing cold air-conditioning. Unfortunately, we discovered later that we should also have paid a visit to the harbor authorities to get our anchoring permit, but because we were leaving the next day, we were hoping it wouldn't matter. Once we were finished with immigration, we walked back into town and stopped at another waterside cafe, this time for a cocktail and some lunch. It was really quite pleasant sitting there watching all the boats go past. An enormous cargo ship passed by that was almost as big as the town itself; it provided quite a spectacle for all us tourists.

After lunch we visited the Curacao boatyard, where we were hoping to have the boat hauled out. Unfortunately, they were fully booked and didn't have any room for us until November. The boatyard was nice and appeared to be very safe, patrolled twenty-four hours a day by security guards with dogs.

We drove around exploring the island for a while before eventually return-ing to the boat. For dinner we took the dinghy across to a little restaurant we had noticed on our way into the harbor that was right in Spanish Waters. The food was quite nice, and the setting was absolutely lovely. My short visit here had dispelled any of the nasty rumors I had heard—I really liked Curacao. I had only experienced a small portion of it, but I would absolutely visit again. It's really quite beautiful. I was sad to be leaving but excited at the prospect of returning to Bonaire.

Oh, little did I know of the forthcoming adventure awaiting me there.

Portobello Mushrooms with Mascarpone, Blue Cheese, and Basil

6 large portobello mushrooms
1½ tablespoons olive oil
¾ cup mascarpone cheese
5 ounces (about ¾ cup) Stilton or other blue cheese, crumbled
½ cup toasted walnuts, roughly chopped
Freshly ground black pepper
½ cup basil leaves, chopped

1. Preheat the oven to 350 degrees F.
2. To clean the mushrooms, wipe them with a damp paper towel, then cut out the stalks. *(Don't wash the mushrooms, or they will become soggy.)*
3. Line a baking tin with foil, brush the foil with the olive oil, and place the mushrooms gill side up.
4. Mix the mascarpone with the blue cheese and walnuts, and season with plenty of pepper.
5. Fill the mushroom caps with the cheese-and-walnut mixture, and sprinkle with chopped basil.
6. Bake for 10 to 15 minutes.
   Serve hot or at room temperature.
   Enjoy.

Moroccan Couscous

1 red bell pepper, seeded and diced
2 yellow onions, chopped
4 medium carrots, finely diced
2 zucchini, finely diced
2 tablespoons olive oil
Sea salt and freshly ground black pepper
1½ cups chicken stock
1½ cups couscous
2 tablespoons unsalted butter
¼ teaspoon ground cumin
½ teaspoon saffron threads, soaked in 1 tablespoon water
2 scallions, chopped

1. Preheat the oven to 375 degrees F.
2. Place the bell peppers, onions, carrots, and zucchini on a baking sheet and toss with the olive oil, 2 teaspoons salt, and 1 teaspoon pepper. Roast for 25 to 30 minutes, turning once, or until all vegetables are tender.
3. In a medium-size saucepan, bring the chicken stock to a boil, and then turn off the heat. Add the couscous, butter, 1 teaspoon salt, ½ teaspoon pepper, cumin, and saffron. Allow to steep for 15 minutes.
4. With a fork, mix the vegetables with the couscous and add the scallions. Serve hot.
   Enjoy.

Chapter 15

Curacao to Bonaire

Coordinates: Curacao 12 7N 68 56'W

Wednesday, September 17

In the morning, Bob and Niki returned the rental car; meanwhile, I prepared the boat for sail. Bob decided it would be a good idea to fix the problem with the auto helm before leaving. It took way longer than expected to fix (nothing new there then). It was approaching midday before we finally motored out of Spanish Waters.

The sail back was lovely (my overactive imagination was able to take a rest). We were into the wind and, fortunately, *Daisy* liked it that way. We arrived back at Bonaire just before sunset and easily picked up a mooring in the bay.

We went ashore for dinner at one of the local Chinese restaurants. The food was not great, but it was lovely spending the evening out with Niki. I just wished we had picked a nice restaurant on the front, where we could have enjoyed the ocean breezes, instead of being in the center of town.

Thursday, September 18

We rented a car, loaded the cooler with drinks, and set off around the island. We drove through the little village of Rincon ("corner" in Spanish), Bonaire's first permanent settlement, founded in the late fifteenth century. Spanish settlers chose the location deep in the island's interior as a safe haven from pirates. Later under the Dutch, Rincon became home to the many slaves who worked on the plantations. Today Rincon is a cluster of pastel cottages, small stores, and streetside cafes and restaurants. It's also the birthplace of many of the island's political and business leaders. On market day, dozens of booths are set up along the main road, selling locally made food and handcrafts, fish, and locally grown fruits and vegetables. There's not much to see here other than on festival days, which apparently occur with amazing frequency.

Our first stop after Rincon was the Bonaire National Marine Park. The park encompasses the entire coast of Bonaire, including Klein Bonaire and Lac Bay. This area is about 2,700 hectares (approximately 6,669 acres) and includes coral reef, sea grass, and mangroves.

Parrots, flamingos, parakeets, and iguanas are only a few of the many endemic species that live within the park. The beaches inside the park are important nesting grounds for the four species of sea turtles found in the Caribbean. They are well protected here, unlike on many of the other Caribbean islands where they have been almost wiped out. We stopped to look around the little museum at the entrance to the park before heading out. I was particularly interested in the history of the island's development. A better understanding of the island's formation explained how it has become such a marine paradise.

We took the long drive around the island, stopping first at Salina Matijs, a large lake where we saw hundreds of flamingos. We were able to get quite close and take photographs. Our next stop was Playa Chikitu, a rocky cove backed by sand dunes and a nesting ground for turtles. We next visited Boka Chikitu, a treasure chest of fossil shells and coral. From there we drove on to Seru Grandi, a high terrace that's about one million years old. Niki and I each built a "spirit hut" by piling small stones on top of each other. Thousands of visitors before us had obviously done the same: there were literally thousands of spirit huts everywhere we looked. Bob had trouble pulling us away from our fun building projects. We continued on to Suplado, better known as "the blow hole." It proved to be a bit of a disappointment because the sea was quite calm, so there were no spectacular splashes to be seen. Poor Niki had developed the most dreadful headache, and, unfortunately, we had nothing to give her.

We continued on to Malmok, the most northern point on Bonaire, and climbed up a steep hill to see the lighthouse. The lighthouse was no longer in use and had been sealed up with concrete to prevent people from entering. The view from the top of the hill, however, definitely made the climb worth the trouble.

As we drove around the island, we saw a multitude of colorful lizards and birds and stopped frequently to get a closer look at them. We drove on to look for a lake called Pos Mangel. We parked the car and walked along the trail leading to the lake. Niki spotted an enormous bees nest that was buzzing noisily with activity; visions of us all running for our lives trailed by a million bees popped into my mind, so we moved hastily along. We eventually came to Pos Mangel, which, probably due to the very dry weather, had sadly shrunk to nothing more than a large puddle. I was concerned about the possibility of mosquitoes and encouraged Bob and Niki to get a move on. A large, inquisitive iguana approached us on the path, obviously looking for food; feeding the iguanas here is prohibited, so we made our way back to the car.

We drove on past the beaches of Boka Bartol and Boka Katuna and stopped to look at Playa Benge, a dive site with a beautiful white sandy beach. The climb to reach the beach looked rather hazardous, so we took some photographs and drove on. We passed the dive sites of Playa Funchi and Bise Morto to stop at Wayaka. That too looked to be a difficult access, so we hurried on to Boka Slagbaai. We needed to get there quickly, because the park rangers move you out at precisely 3:30 p.m., and it was at least an hour's drive back to the entrance of the park. Niki's headache had become so bad now, she was feeling quite sick. We stopped at Slagbaai, where there was an open bar with a few people around. We asked if anyone had anything for headaches, and luckily an older English gentleman obliged us with some aspirin.

Slagbaai is a beautiful beach with historic buildings and a picnic area. The snorkeling looked great, but we didn't have time to indulge; the rangers arrived five minutes after we did to move everyone on. So we piled into our vehicle and headed back. The roads around the park were not so much roads as rough, rocky clearings through cactus forests. There were huge boulders and rocks, potholes, and dead cactus branches littering the path. It was an unbelievably bumpy, rough ride that shook the car violently and tossed us out of our seats several times. The drive did not help poor Nicolette's headache at all, and we had to pull over several times so she could get out; she felt so sick.

We stopped in Rincon to try and get Niki something to eat. Sadly, at the only open food service we could find, the server didn't speak any English, and the food didn't look very appetizing. We decided to wait until we got back to the boat to eat. By the time we were back on *Daisy*, the aspirin tablets had kicked in, and Nicolette was feeling much better.

Friday, September 19

Niki stayed on board to sketch while Bob drove me to the supermarket. I shopped while he went to immigration to check Nicolette and himself out. Sadly for me, they were both flying back to the States in two days. Later that afternoon, we moved *Daisy* back to Village Harbor Marina and came alongside with ease. We managed to get tied off just before the heavy rain started.

Saturday, September 20

Bob had arranged for another rental car, so we left early to get to the Washington Slagbaai National Park. I packed a small picnic and plenty of drinks in the cooler. This time we took the short route through the park, which was bumpier (if that was possible) than the long route we had taken on Thursday. We stopped first at Wayaka, where we climbed down to the beach with our snorkel gear. It was a small, shallow lagoon and the water didn't look very inviting, so we decided to drive on to Slagbaai. As we were getting back in the car, two Danish people on mountain bikes stopped to say hello; I had to admire their stamina and fitness cycling through this park—driving through was hard enough.

We drove on to Slagbaai. There were a couple of other cars and families there, so we went to the far end of the beach where it was quiet. Niki and I collected shells before swimming. The snorkeling was wonderful, with an abundance of fish, in particular several different species of large parrot fish. There was a spectacular garden of coral with a lovely spotted filefish and enormous tube worms in vibrant colors. We ate our picnic lunch in the shade then packed up and headed back to *Daisy* for a shower and a short rest before returning ashore. We drove out through town and past the airport to look at the houses along the seafront. We walked around for a while and came across a new construction. The contemporary-style home, very fitting for Bonaire, had the most incredible views over the ocean as well as a good-size patio and the beginnings of a swimming pool. I definitely could imagine myself living there. I closed my eyes and pictured myself sitting alongside my swimming pool, sipping a cocktail while looking out at the turquoise blue sea. One can but dream!

We drove back into town and had a cocktail at a seafront restaurant called Salsa. We had planned to take Nicolette to Mona Lisa for dinner, but the restaurant was closed on weekends, so we went instead to La Gurelana on the front and enjoyed a delicious dinner while watching the sunset. I felt quite sad, knowing both Niki and Bob were leaving the next day, and I would be alone here for three weeks.

Sunday, September 21

I woke at 4 a.m. to take Nicolette to the airport and then at 6:30 a.m. drove back to the airport to drop off Bob. I returned to the boat to spend the rest of the day doing laundry and cleaning. I was alone now until Bob was due to return in three weeks.

In all honesty, despite being in such a beautiful location, I was not thrilled at the prospect of three weeks alone in Bonaire. I didn't know anyone there. Only a couple of other boats in the harbor were occupied at that time, and the people spoke very little English. Although they were all very pleasant, no one bothered with me other than a polite greeting as they passed by. It was a very lonely time for me. I've really never minded my own company, but in Bonaire there was no choice other than to be alone.

The time Bob was away dragged by slowly and wasn't helped by the fact that I injured my back. I had been sitting and drinking a cup of tea on deck one afternoon when a lady off another boat walked by and called out *bon bini* (a Dutch greeting meaning "hello" or "welcome"). I twisted around to return the greeting when a sudden sharp pain shot from my spine down to my knee. The next four days were probably the most miserable days I've ever spent. I was completely unable to move without pain. I couldn't even climb onto the bed, so I slept on the hard salon floor. Any movement caused excruciating pains in my back, so needless to say I didn't do much for four days. The only relief I could find was lying on my back on the hard floor. I didn't want my family to worry about me, so each night when I talked to them on Skype, I put on a brave face and lied about my wonderful days. At the end of each call, I would collapse in tears. Four days after my injury, my back started to improve, and each day it improved a little more. By the time Bob returned, I was almost back to normal. I was looking forward to spending time with him, touring the island again, and snorkeling off the wonderful beaches. Little did I know there was something else in store for me in Bonaire.

[Cook's note]

This is one of my absolute favorite summer salads: delicious, refreshing, and so quick and easy to put together.

Chicken Waldorf Salad

Dressing:
1 cup pineapple juice
1 cup apple juice
Juice and zest of 1 large lemon
1 cup mayonnaise
2 tablespoons pure honey
1 tablespoon whole-grain Dijon mustard
1 teaspoon Coleman's English dry mustard
½ teaspoon turmeric
½ cup olive oil
Salt and freshly ground black pepper

Salad:
1 whole rotisserie chicken, diced
2 Granny Smith apples, cored and diced
1½ cups red seedless grapes, halved
1 cup celery, chopped
½ cup scallions, chopped
1 cup walnuts, toasted
½ cup pumpkin seeds, toasted

1. Pour the pineapple juice and the apple juice in a heavy medium-size saucepan.
2. Boil until the juices coat the back of a spoon and are reduced to ⅔ cup, about 10 minutes. Let cool completely.
3. In a medium bowl, whisk lemon juice, zest, mayonnaise, honey, mustards, and turmeric. Gradually whisk in juice mixture, then oil. Season with salt and pepper.
4. Add the diced chicken, apples, grapes, celery, scallions, walnuts, and pumpkin seeds. Toss well to coat in the sauce.
   Serve with a green salad and slices of a freshly baked baguette.
   Enjoy.

[Cook's note]

If you like blue cheese, you will love this coleslaw: it goes great with any salad or cold dish. It's sweet, salty, and savory all at the same time.

Blue Cheese Coleslaw with Dried Cranberries

½ green cabbage
½ red cabbage
½ red onion
4 large carrots
2 cups mayonnaise
¼ cup Dijon mustard
2 tablespoons whole-grain mustard
2 tablespoons apple cider vinegar
½ teaspoon sea salt
½ teaspoon freshly ground black pepper
1½ cups crumbled Roquefort
½ cup dried cranberries, sweetened
1 cup fresh cilantro, chopped

1. Finely shred all the vegetables and place them in a large bowl.
2. Whisk together the remaining ingredients, except the Roquefort, cranberries, and cilantro.
3. Pour the sauce mix into the bowl with the shredded vegetables and stir to thoroughly coat them.
4. Toss the Roquefort, cranberries, and cilantro into the vegetables; keep a little cilantro aside for garnish.
5. Cover and refrigerate for at least 1 hour before serving.
   Enjoy.

[Cook's note]

When I was growing up, my nan would make this trifle every Sunday; it was something I looked forward to all week. You can make it without the sherry and the rum if you don't like alcohol, but I think it's the sherry that makes it so special. I changed the peaches in her original recipe to mangos; either will work equally well. The liquid in the canned fruit helps the jelly (or Jell-O) set, according to Nan.

Great Grandma's Very Sherry Tipsy Trifle

½ cup strawberry jam
2 tablespoons rum
Jam roll sponge, cut into 1-inch-thick slices (or 1 pound cake)
½ cup Harvey's Bristol Cream sherry
1 packet strawberry Jell-O mix
1 14-ounce can (tin) sliced mangos in their juice
1 pint frozen strawberries, thawed and drained

Topping:
2 tablespoons slivered almonds, toasted
1 tablespoon desiccated, sweetened coconut, toasted
1 cup heavy cream
Fresh sliced strawberries and fresh mint leaves, for garnish

1. In a small bowl, mix the strawberry jam with the rum. Spread the mix over the sponge slices. Layer the bottom of a fruit bowl with the sponge slices. Pour the sherry over the sponge slices.
2. Make the Jell-O according to the package instructions, but drain the juice from the tinned mangos to add to the liquid.
3. Layer the strawberries and mango slices over the sponge. Pour the Jell-O over the fruit and sponge slices. Allow it to cool. Refrigerate for a couple of hours, until the Jell-O sets.
4. Meanwhile, toast the almonds and coconut in a dry nonstick pan over medium heat, just until they start to turn golden. Set aside to cool.
5. Whip the cream until it forms soft peaks. Cover the cold trifle with the cream. Sprinkle the toasted almonds and coconut over the cream. Decorate with the remaining strawberries and mint leaves.
    Refrigerate until ready to serve.
    Enjoy.

Chapter 16

Hurricane Omar, Bonaire

Tuesday, October 14

We were still alongside in the Village Harbor Marina, Bonaire. Bob had returned after eighteen days on business back in the States. We busily cleaned, polished, and did general boat maintenance in preparation for the trip back to Curacao, where *Daisy* was due to be hauled out of the water for a few months for her annual maintenance checks and repainting of the hull.

The weather was typically fabulous for the Caribbean that time of year. And in this area well out of the hurricane zone, thoughts of tropical storms and hurricanes were not exactly at the forefront of our minds. Bob had noted a small tropical wave headed our way, but it was nothing to cause us concern: it hadn't formed into anything resembling a storm and obviously had no patterns resembling a hurricane, because you don't get hurricanes this far south. Or do you?

In the early hours, we were woken by a light sprinkling of rain coming through the open hatch in our cabin.

We performed the usual manic scrabble to secure all the open hatches and portholes then returned to bed. Within minutes, the wind had reached near gale-force proportions, and the gentle sprinkling of rain had turned into a torrential downpour. Unusually, the wind appeared to be coming from a westerly direction. This ridiculous wind seemed to be following us. This was not the first time we had been caught unaware by these unusual wind changes in this part of the Caribbean. We quickly donned our foul-weather gear and braved the weather to check on the security of the lines. Once we had secured everything, we put out extra fenders and then retreated below to comfort and shelter from the storm.

Daisy shifted uncomfortably in her slip throughout the night as the surge increased. The wind continued to howl, and the rain hammered down relentlessly. It proved a good test for leaks, which we were happy to discover we didn't have. But I couldn't help worrying about *Whoops-a-Daisy*, which I had left tied only by the painter to the side of the boat. At first light we braved the weather to once again check the lines and the dinghy, which was bouncing around noisily. I was relieved to see it miraculously still tied alongside. Bob had deliberately left enough slack for *Daisy* to rise with the surge, but the poor little dinghy was half submerged and completely full of water. The wind and rain had eased a little, enabling me to make a precarious climb into the dinghy and bale out without getting thoroughly drenched or washed overboard in the process.

The strong wind continued to blow from the west, pushing *Daisy* hard against the concrete dock, and she was moving considerably with the surge. Bob decided we should check the lines on the unoccupied boat in the slip alongside us. It was a much larger and heavier boat than *Daisy*. Upon inspection, we discovered to our horror that the neighboring boat's lines were stretched dangerously taut and were close to breaking. One of her deck cleats had been partially pulled out— the situation looked grim. Bob was extremely concerned for the security of the neighboring boat: the surge had raised the level of water in the marina so much that her lines were actually sawing down through her deck. It was only a matter of time before she would break free, which would send her crashing into us. Despite our best efforts, we were unable to ease the lines, which were pulled so tight we could not free up even the first quarter of an inch of wiggle room. We knew that if left to its own devices—either due to the lines severing or the attachment points breaking free as the deck disintegrated—the seventy-ton vessel was quickly going to become an oversized bull in our very small china shop! And we were first in line for a visit.

In poor light, as the wind howled and the rain stung our eyes and blurred our vision, we set about adding more lines in an attempt to ease the tension on the current lines. Our crazy scheme was to create enough compressive forces on the yacht to haul it down against its buoyancy and enable us to loosen the piano wires that once had been braided shorelines. (Quite obviously, this was all Bob's idea; I just wanted to run for the hills.)

We ran a line under the dodger to the winch in the cockpit. We looped a line around the main mast, tied another from the anchor windlass to the dock, and finally tied one more to a large powered winch that ran the line through what looked like hefty spinnaker pulleys aft of the cockpit. We were both aware of the danger: A wrong move or loose loop of line that trapped a hand, foot, or limb between the fixed dock and the writhing giant would cause severe injury, even amputation. My imagination was moving at triple warp speed, giving me quite a headache. I had to keep silently reminding myself of how much I loved boat life. Finally, cold, wet, tired, and out of both ideas and suitable spare lines, we had to see if we could overcome Samuel Plimsoll's theories about how low a vessel was meant to float in the water (again, all Bob's idea).

To our immense relief, the arrangement appeared to be working! The winches inched the vessel over, probably tilting it in the water more than pulling it lower, but who cares about the accuracy of the science? We (well, Bob) finally exerted enough tension to ease the pressure on the original lines and, much to our relief, were able to loosen them to prevent further carnage to the deck. We set about reorganizing the lines to release the pent-up destructive forces and also to have the ability to compensate for further surge in the water level. Relief flowed over us, and no vote was needed to decide the next move. We slipped and splashed our way back to the security of *Daisy*, knowing that once again we could leave the elements to do their worst, while we would be secure in the warm, dry confines of our floating refuge (hmmm).

Throughout the day, the skies remained as dark as night, and the near gale-force winds blew incessantly. The harbor was quickly filling with boats previously on moorings in the bay as well as other boats in the vicinity seeking refuge from the storm. The marina staff was busy squeezing boats into every available space, rafting one boat to the next. The scene was one of frenzied activity. At 11 pm, Omar officially became a category 1 hurricane (oh, crap!).

Wednesday, October 15

After another thoroughly restless night, daylight brought stormy skies, black with rain. We watched with disappointment as the wind and rain continued their relentless abuse. Concern for the security of our neighboring boat, which had posed such a threat to us, forced us back up on deck. While Bob checked the other boat's lines, I once again baled out *Whoops-a-Daisy*, a thankless task: I knew only too well the dinghy would be full again within the hour. Through our large cabin windows we could see the masts of the boats in the harbor swaying to and fro dangerously close to one another.

Always the alarmist, I pictured masts crashing into each other, tangled lines, broken spreaders, and torn-off boat parts being hurled about like missiles in the wind. There was nothing more we could do but stay below, out of harm's way. I busied myself baking scones, drinking cups of tea, and watching an entire series of *CSI* on television; murder and intrigue proved to be an effective distraction from the mayhem that was taking place outside. By nightfall, the wind was still blowing, but with much less ferocity than during the day. For the first time in almost thirty-six hours, I didn't have to worry about being crushed by the neighboring boat paying us an unwelcome visit or being smacked in the head by flying debris when I ventured up on deck. The rain had finally abated, and it wasn't long before we opened the hatches and let some air back into the boat.

Thursday, October 16

At last, an uninterrupted night's sleep. Through our cabin hatch we could see beautiful blue sky. People in the surrounding boats were peering out from their hatches and cockpits like meerkats in the desert. There were one or two black clouds on the horizon, but nothing that looked threatening. As the day progressed, the weather improved, even bringing with it some brilliant sunshine. One almost had to wonder, had there really been a storm? Looking back I realized it wasn't the weather that scared me so much as the very real threat of being crushed by the neighboring boat. Fortunately, we all survived

The normally crystal clear water around Bonaire's coastline was gray, murky, and angry looking, with tons of debris floating everywhere. The pier where we had previously spent so many happy cocktail hours had been demolished; all that remained were a few broken concrete pillars. There was substantial damage to the shoreline roads, with large craters full of water and uprooted trees all along the seafront. But already the cleanup was underway.

At the end of October 2008, Bob and I took *Daisy* back to the Curacao Marine boatyard, where she was taken out of the water to have her bottom painted and other maintenance work done. At the beginning of November, we flew back to the States for a few months.

Bob returned to work on the boat many times during her stay at the Curacao boatyard, but I didn't return to *Daisy* until June 2009.

My last month aboard *Daisy* had not been a pleasant one, and I was both excited and relieved to be leaving her and returning to dry land. The original plan had been for me to return to Ohio for a couple of months, but I had quite defiantly managed to delay my return, spending almost seven months back on land. I was in seventh heaven: shopping for fresh fruit and vegetables, cooking fancy dishes, taking long hot showers or baths (oh, the utter bliss of taking a bath!), walking Danni's little dog by the lake, playing with the horses at the barn, and spending hours browsing at my favorite store, Barnes and Noble.

I had my first Christmas at home in seven years. Before we owned *Daisy*, we had taken almost every Christmas on a charter boat in the Caribbean. Maybe because I'm a Christmas baby (born December 20), I found myself craving frosty mornings, snowfalls, and log fires. Unfortunately, Bob did not share my delight at being off the boat: he hated the cold weather and couldn't wait to get back. He's really only happy when at sea, whereas, sadly, my few years at sea had proven beyond a shadow of a doubt that I am most definitely a landlubber.

[Cook's note]

The first time I made this cheesecake (about thirty years ago) my husband said it was the most delicious cheesecake he had ever eaten. It's the dense, stick-to-the-roof-of-your-mouth kind, which is how we like our cheesecake. None of this lighter-than-air nonsense—this is the real deal. Of course, thirty years ago Bob and I were both slim and fit and easily able to work off the calories; today it's a different story. This is absolutely a special-occasion cheesecake for holidays, birthdays, special family gatherings, or maybe something to indulge in when life is just throwing you a curveball.

Daisy's Rib-Sticking Caribbean Cheesecake

Base:
6 tablespoons unsalted butter, melted
6 ounces (3 cups) digestive biscuits (or graham crackers), crushed
2 tablespoons raw cane sugar

Filling:
3 (8-ounce packets) full-fat cream cheese
½ cup plus 2 teaspoons fine white sugar
3 large free-range eggs, separated
1 tablespoon cornstarch, mixed with 2 tablespoons freshly squeezed lemon juice
1 teaspoon lemon zest
1 cup sour cream
Seeds scraped from 2 vanilla pods
Pulp from 3 passion fruits

1. Preheat the oven to 350 degrees F.
2. Grease a 9-inch loose-bottom (or springform) cake pan with 1 teaspoon unsalted butter.
3. In a medium-size bowl, combine the crushed biscuits (or graham crackers) with the sugar and melted butter.
4. Spoon the mixture into the base of a cake pan and press it down firmly.
5. In a large mixing bowl, combine the cream cheese and sugar; add the egg yolks and beat with electric hand mixer until smooth. Stir in the cornstarch mix and lemon zest.

6. In another large mixing bowl, beat the egg whites until stiff, about 2 to 4 minutes. Fold the egg whites gently into the cream cheese mixture.

7. Spoon the mixture into the cake pan.

8. Bake in the center of the oven for 20 minutes, or until the center of the cheesecake feels firm when pressed.

9. Meanwhile, in a small mixing bowl combine the sour cream, sugar, and vanilla seeds.

10. Remove the cake pan from the oven. Using a palette knife, gently spread the cream mix over the top.

11. Place the cheesecake back in the oven for 5 more minutes, then remove it from the oven and set it aside to cool.

12. When cool, remove the cheesecake from the pan and refrigerate it until ready to serve.

To serve: top with the passion fruit or a selection of fresh berries.

Enjoy.

[Cook' note]

OK, so this recipe bakes for over an hour, which is much longer than I usually cook anything when on board, bearing in mind one is supposed to be frugal with the gas. There are times, however, when you're alongside and can easily refill the gas tanks, so use that time to try this recipe, and I promise you will love it. It's also a useful recipe to keep handy because you'll be surprised how many almost-black bananas you'll have on board—this is the best way to use them. By microwaving the bananas first and then reducing the liquid that's released, you'll find that it really concentrates the flavor; it makes the most moist and delicious, richly flavored banana bread ever. I especially love this bread because it smells like Christmas cake.

Banana, Walnut, Date and Honey Bread

5 very ripe bananas
1½ cups all-purpose flour
1 teaspoon baking soda
¼ teaspoon grated nutmeg
¼ teaspoon ground cloves
8 tablespoons (1 stick) salted butter, softened
½ cup walnuts, chopped and toasted
½ cup dates, pitted and chopped
½ cup light brown sugar
2 teaspoons lemon zest
3 large free-range eggs
2 tablespoons pure honey
2 tablespoons good rum (optional)

1. Preheat the oven to 350 degrees F.
2. Grease a 2-pound loaf tin (pan).
3. Microwave the bananas for about 5 minutes to release their liquid; drain in a strainer for about 10 minutes. (You should have about ½ to ¾ cup of liquid.)
4. In a small saucepan over medium heat, reduce the liquid from the bananas to about ¼ cup; allow it to cool for about 10 minutes.
5. Add the cooled liquid to the bananas, and mash to a pulp.

6. In a large bowl, mix the sugar, flour and baking soda with the nutmeg and cloves. Rub the butter into the flour until it resembles fine breadcrumbs.
7. Stir in the walnuts, dated, bananas, lemon zest, eggs, and honey.
8. Pour the mix into the loaf tin and bake for about 1¼ hours, or until a toothpick comes out clean.
9. Cover the loaf tin with aluminum foil toward the end of cooking (about the last 15 minutes) to prevent the edges from burning.
10. Once the loaf is cool, turn upside down, and using a skewer punch holes evenly over the base of the loaf, then drizzle the rum over the base of the loaf (the holes will allow the rum to easily seep into the loaf). Wrap in baking parchment, then in tin foil, and leaving the loaf upside down, set aside for 2 – 3 hours.

To serve, brush warm honey over the top of bread.

Enjoy.

Chapter 17

Curacao to Aruba

Coordinates: 3 Aruba 12 30'N 69 58'W

Thursday, June 29, 2009

Bob and I spent twelve days at Curacao Marine, cleaning, varnishing, provisioning, and generally getting *Daisy* ready for her trip to Aruba. It was extremely hot and dusty working at the boatyard, but the pleasant staff was always on hand when we needed anything. The Budget Marine store on-site also proved very useful.

I loved grocery shopping in Curacao. The supermarkets were almost as well stocked as those on mainland America, so it was not usually a problem finding ingredients that were often hard to come by throughout the rest of the Caribbean.

We got to know most of the other yachties, a friendly group, stranded like us at the boatyard. Some people on another Oyster just down the dock from *Daisy* invited us over for dinner, which was lovely since we were so busy preparing to sail, I hadn't had time to even think about dinner. They served the most delicious pasta in a creamy mushroom sauce, along with some wonderful wine. It made a very pleasant change to relax and enjoy a social evening with our new friends.

Tuesday, July 7

We pulled out of the boatyard at 6:30 a.m. and had a quiet sail with a mere 14 knots of wind and a rolly sea. We motor sailed all the way, with just the jib out, and arrived at Oranjestad at 4:30 p.m., only to be told by the customs and immigration officer over the VHF officer we had to go back to Barcadera to check in. Bob was worried about making it to Barcadera and then back to Oranjestad before running out of daylight, because we were unfamiliar with the Oranjestad Renaissance Marina, where we had to come alongside. But the customs officer would not give in, so we turned around and motored back to Barcadera, where we were directed to come alongside in a space about half *Daisy*'s length. We circled around for about twenty minutes, looking for a possible space to pull up, with the customs officer standing on the dock waving his arms in frustration. He kept insisting that we pull into the tiny space. I was totally confused: Did he think Bob was David Copperfield and could just magically reduce *Daisy*'s size from sixty feet to thirty feet? How he thought we were going to fit in, I have no idea. Eventually we pulled up alongside a fishing boat and rafted *Daisy* to her with the help of the fishermen.

Bob climbed from *Daisy* into the fishing boat and ashore to the customs office to check in. Each port offered its different challenges, and this one was proving to be no different.

I gave the fishermen beer as a thank you for their help, which they all happily accepted. They were busily chattering away to me in rapid Spanish. I didn't understand a word, so I just smiled and laughed when they did. For all I knew they were laughing at me, but as long as we were able to check in, I was happy to be the butt of their amusement. I really should learn to speak the language; my knowledge of French is pretty redundant out here.

While Bob was checking us in, I was entertained by the antics and aerial acrobatics of a flock of gigantic frigate birds circling above *Daisy* and the fishing boat. Watching these incredible birds so closely, I was amazed at their sheer size: I knew they're capable of seven-foot wingspans, but up close they appeared so much larger.

We arrived back at the Renaissance Marina, also known as Seaport, with less than an hour of daylight left and came alongside with the help of Sanders, the marina manager. We were right on the end of the dock alongside the resort's casino. Fortunately for Bob, I'm not a gambler, so the casino would not be drawing me in.

Aruba is the smallest of the ABC islands, at just 19 miles long and 7 miles across at its widest point; it's safely located on the southern edge of the hurricane belt and enjoys almost perfect weather year-round. The northwestern side of the island is made up of pristine white sandy beaches that rank as some of the most beautiful in the world. The turquoise blue sea is calm, with visibility in some areas of up to 100 feet. In contrast, the craggy northeast coast is wild and rugged, with huge waves crashing along its coast, throwing spray into the air up to fifty feet and higher. The interior is desertlike, similar to to Bonaire, with cactus, scrub, and rock formations. Like Bonaire, it, too, is incredibly hot and horribly humid.

Aruba is very well-known for aloe, which was introduced to the island from the Mediterranean in 1850; the plant thrived so well in the dry climate that Aruba quickly became one of the world's largest exporters of aloe. A large selection of locally made aloe products is available from a number of shops throughout the island.

Once we had secured the boat, we both showered and changed, and then walked to the shops and restaurants. We enjoyed a pleasant meal and a bottle of wine. Aruba did not appear to be as expensive as the other islands; the prices here were similar to those in the States. On the other hand, Aruba's luxurious duty-free shops offered all the designer fashions and diamonds you could ever want.

Thursday, July 10

My good friend Angie arrived for a seven-day visit. I had been so looking forward to her coming; we always manage to have tons of fun when we're together. Bob was returning to the States on business for a couple of weeks, so it was going to be just Angie and me—and this provided me with an excellent excuse not to work. We intended to have a week of fun and really get to know the island of Aruba.

I was eager to show Angie the Renaissance's two beautiful swimming pools overlooking the ocean this side of the harbor. It also operates a complimentary boat from the dock for hotel and marina guests to travel across to the private island resort.

We packed our suntan lotion, snorkeling gear, and reading material and headed over to the island. The island provided complimentary beach towels and sun beds. There were two beaches: a family beach and a topless beach. Seven flamingos resided at the topless beach and were extraordinarily tame; Angie and I watched them strut proudly along the beach between the sunbathing tourists. We found some fish food in a dispenser and offered it to the flamingos, who happily ate out of our hands. (Oh, and just in case you were worried about the two of us choosing the topless beach, I can assure you we were both respectably attired in swimsuits. I can't speak for Angie, but my topless days on the beach ended about thirty years ago.)

Besides flamingos, Aruba is also famous for its iguanas. They were everywhere you looked, both on the mainland and on the private island. Many of the larger iguanas could be seen by the boat dock, where the hotel staff fed them at midday.

We were both very keen to see more of the island, so Angie decided to rent a car for a couple of days. We planned to set off up the coast to Palm Beach on a sightseeing expedition.

Now I said car, but a more accurate description would be a multishaded, luminous yellow wobbly tin box about the size of an armchair that rattled and squeaked loudly—a delightful, attention-grabbing idiosyncrasy that we would happily have done without. Having said that, the squeak perfectly fit the personality of the vehicle (and I use the word vehicle with reservation). But Angie wanted to look at the time-share apartments at Palm Beach, and because *she* had rented the car and was doing the driving, who was I to argue? I was just along for the ride. Eager to get started, I grabbed the door handle to open the passenger door, and it came right off in my hand! Angie opened the door for me, and I got in and threw the handle into the glove box. At least I wouldn't have to worry about locking the door when I got out.

It was a lovely sunny afternoon in Aruba as the two of us squeaked and rattled our way up the coast. The resorts at Palm Beach were literally crawling with thousands of tourists. The beaches were all much too busy for my liking. As I mentioned before, having been thoroughly spoiled by all the beautiful, isolated beaches I've become accustomed to since living on *Daisy*, I don't cope at all well with crowds. Similarly unimpressed, and to my immense relief, Angie suggested we move on. We made our way back to our dinky little yellow peril that we had left parked behind a garbage can in the far corner of the parking lot.

We had no idea where we were going, so we just headed farther up the coast. My imagination had kicked in again, this time not with fear but with curiosity: I was wondering how many (and what) bits were falling off our attention-grabbing excuse for a vehicle as we squeaked, bounced, and rattled along the bumpy roads.

We stopped along with coachloads of tourists at the California Lighthouse, which towers above the craggy Noord, on the hilltop of Hudishibana. From this location, the views across the island were absolutely stunning.

Angie and I decided to spoil ourselves and have lunch at the Italian restaurant next to the lighthouse, La Trattoria el Faro Blanco. There were spectacular views over the ocean from the restaurant's outdoor terraces. Both the upper and lower terraces were covered, providing diners with welcome shade. There was also a garden terrace, but with the blistering heat in Aruba, I wouldn't imagine the garden terrace got much use during the day.

We both enjoyed a delicious, relaxing lunch at our table overlooking the garden terrace with a magnificent panorama to the ocean beyond. Sitting there at our white-linen-covered table, sipping wine, and enjoying the gentle breeze in the lovely, quiet atmosphere of the pretty restaurant felt quite special. I was thoroughly enjoying the day. After lunch we set off once again around the island. We managed to get lost more than once, but we did stumble across an ostrich farm, a donkey sanctuary, and the beautiful Arikok National Park, which was getting ready to open in a couple of weeks. We saw many of Aruba's famous divi-divi trees. Bent almost in half by the northeasterly trade winds, they looked like nature's signposts, all pointing southwest.

That evening as we drove back up the coast to Palm Beach looking for somewhere to have dinner, we came across an absolutely fabulous hotel, which for legal reasons (that will become apparent later) I will decline to name. Angie parked the yellow peril behind a small bush at the side of the hotel; we didn't feel that our current mode of transport necessarily fit in with the image of the grand hotel and, therefore, didn't quite warrant valet parking. We applied lipstick, brushed our hair, straightened our clothes, and casually waltzed through the sun-drenched entrance of the lobby, looking as bored and expensive as we possibly could. Angie always tells me, "Act like you belong," when the two of us are tricking our way into places we're not supposed to be, like the private lounges in the airports. (Just kidding. Um, forget I said that.)

By any standard, the hotel had a magnificent foyer, with marble floors, enormous floral arrangements, uniformed doormen, and incredibly ornate decor. Impressive. We walked casually around the hotel, stopping to read the menus that were displayed outside the many elegant restaurants within the hotel. There were no prices listed: each menu may as well have read, "You can't afford to eat here, so piss off." With heads held high, we made our way to the terrace. "Cocktails?" Angie inquired. "Lovely," I replied.

We found a table for two overlooking the hotel pool and beautifully manicured gardens with an uninterrupted view to the turquoise ocean beyond. It was perfect timing: it was just approaching sunset. We sank back in our comfy chairs as the waitress approached and asked what we would like to drink. "A glass of Chardonnay, please," Angie said. "Merlot for me," I added with a smile. Within a couple of minutes, she was back with our drinks. The wine was outstandingly good—too good. We looked wide-eyed at each other over the rim of the glasses as we took our first sip. I could almost see the dollar signs reflected in Angie's eyes. "I think this is going to be expensive," I whispered, not to be overheard by the people at the next table. "You think?" Angie replied, raising one eyebrow. Well the damage was done, so we just decided to sit back, enjoy the wine and the sunset, and wait for the bill.

Unfortunately, the bill didn't arrive, but the headwaiter and the bar manager did. "May we see your wristbands please?" asked the waiter. "Wristbands?" I repeated stupidly. "Yes, your wristbands. You are guests here at the hotel, aren't you?" the waiter asked. Dumbfounded, Angie and I looked at each other. "No, we just came in for a drink. Is there a problem?" Angie said. The waiter and the manager turned and looked at each other openmouthed. "You're not supposed to be here: this is a private all-inclusive hotel," the bar manager said turning to me. "Oh, well, we didn't know. I'm very sorry," I stammered. "If we could just pay for our drinks, we'll leave." I smiled at them while reaching for my purse, but they didn't smile back. "We don't take cash. Only the hotel casino takes cash," the manager stated. I noticed that they were both starting to look a little red-faced and angry, as well as frustrated. "Well, can we pay at the casino?" I inquired. The waiter returned an angry look and replied, "No, the drinks came from the bar here." Angie responded, with just a touch of sarcasm, "Well, the drinks are in our stomachs now, so what would you suggest we do?" The waiter and manager stood there looking at each other in bewilderment. Obviously, we had provided them with an unexpected conundrum. "Well, if we can't pay you, perhaps we should just leave quietly," I whispered, reaching for my bag and standing up. Angie did the same, and before the two men had a chance to respond, the two of us moved swiftly but elegantly (I might add) toward the exit without once looking back. Upon reaching the foyer, we ran, giggling like schoolgirls, out to the yellow peril, lurking where we had left it behind a bush. We jumped in and made a hasty, if not somewhat noisy, getaway.

During the rest of the week, Angie and I made a few more trips to the private resort island to visit the flamingos, soak up the sun, swim, and just relax—it was quite simply a wonderful week.

As a generous thank-you gift, Angie treated me to one of Aruba's main tourist attractions: a submarine ride. When she told me she had booked the trip as a surprise, I was quite worried: I sometimes suffer with claustrophobia, and the idea of being enclosed in a small space with fifty people 130 feet below the surface of the ocean had my imagination running and screaming for the hills. Angie had spent a lot of money on the tickets, however, and it was actually something I had always wanted to do. I just never had the guts to go ahead and actually do it. This was my chance.

As it turned out, the ride was fantastic. We managed to secure seats right at the front next to the pilot, or captain, or whatever he's called, so we had windows to our left and in front. I've discovered that with Angie we always manage to get the best seats, spot, or location—she has a gift.

Once we were all aboard and the submarine hatch was sealed, we very slowly started our descent to 130 feet below. I felt the hairs on the back of my neck prickle with anticipation or maybe it was fear, I'm not quite sure which, but the view was fantastic. We proceeded to crawl along the seabed, alongside a shipwreck, before turning and coming back the same way, ensuring everyone got a really good view of both the reef and the wreck. The marine life and coral reef were quite impressive, and I saw some of the largest barracuda I've ever seen. I was so mesmerized by the reef that I totally forgot about where I was. The submarine excursion was a thoroughly enjoyable trip, and I would highly recommend it to any island visitor who is interested in marine life.

It was a sad day for me when it came time for Angie to leave. We had enjoyed so many fun times together during the week, and I was really going to miss her. I found myself on my own again until Bob returned with Niki.

Crab Ravioli in a Lemon Cream Lobster Sauce

8 ounces precooked crabmeat
1 tablespoon fresh tarragon, chopped
1 tablespoon chives, chopped
1 fresh red chili pepper, seeded and chopped
½ teaspoon lemon grass *(I use Gourmet Garden Lemon-Grass Herb Blend, available in the fresh herb section of most good supermarkets.)*
½ teaspoon freshly ground black pepper
¼ teaspoon Maldon sea salt flakes
1 tablespoon mascarpone cheese
Pinch of paprika
1 packet of wonton wrappers
Milk

1. Mix all ingredients (except wonton wrappers and milk) together in a medium-size bowl.
2. Brush one wonton wrapper lightly with the milk. Place 1 teaspoon of the crab mix in the center of the wonton. Place another wonton wrapper over the top, and press the edges firmly together to make a sealed package.
3. Repeat until all the crab is used.
4. Cover and place the ravioli in the refrigerator while you make the sauce.

Lemon Cream Lobster Sauce:

2 tablespoons unsalted butter
1 level tablespoon all-purpose flour
1 cup 2-percent milk
¾ cup heavy cream
1 tablespoon mascarpone cheese
Zest and juice of 1 lemon
8 ounces cooked lobster meat
½ teaspoon Maldon sea salt flakes
½ teaspoon freshly ground black pepper
Chopped parsley, for garnish

1. Melt the butter in a heavy medium-size saucepan over medium heat. When the butter has melted, remove it from the heat and, using a wooden spoon, stir in the flour. Gradually add the milk, stirring well, and return to the heat.
2. Reduce the heat to low and simmer for 5 to 6 minutes, stirring continuously. Add the cream and the mascarpone, and mix well to combine. Stir in the lemon zest, lemon juice, and lobster meat. Season with salt and pepper.
3. Transfer the sauce to a liquidizer (or blender) and buzz well to make a creamy sauce. Return the sauce to the pan and reduce the heat to the lowest setting. Keep warm while you cook the ravioli.
4. Bring a large pan of salted water to a rolling boil. Drop the ravioli into the water in small batches, and cook for 2 minutes or until the ravioli rise to the surface. Remove with a slotted spoon and transfer to the sauce. Repeat until all the ravioli are cooked.
5. Divide the ravioli equally among the serving plates, and sprinkle with the chopped parsley. Serve immediately.
   Enjoy.

Daisy's Cream-Filled Ginger Nut Cookies

4 ounces self-rising flour
½ level teaspoon bicarbonate of soda
1½ level teaspoons ground ginger
½ level teaspoon ground cinnamon
¼ teaspoon grated nutmeg
¼ teaspoon ground cloves
2 teaspoons fine sugar
4 tablespoons salted butter
3 ounces golden syrup (available in the international aisle of most supermarkets, in the English section)

Filling:
3 cups confectioners' sugar
¼ teaspoon ground cinnamon
4 tablespoons unsalted butter, softened to room temperature
1-inch piece fresh ginger, peeled

1. Preheat the oven to 375 degrees F.
2. Lightly grease two large baking trays and line with baking parchment.
3. Sift the flour, bicarbonate of soda, ginger, cinnamon, nutmeg, and cloves into a small bowl; add the sugar and stir to mix.
4. In a small pan, melt the butter, being careful not to burn it. Stir in the syrup. With a wooden spoon, stir the butter and syrup into the dry ingredients.
5. Using your hands, shape the mix into a thick sausage shape, then cut it into 24 even pieces. Roll each piece into a small ball. Set the balls well apart on the baking trays and flatten slightly.
6. Bake just above the center rack of the oven for about 15 minutes, or until the tops have cracked and are golden brown. Cool for a few minutes on the baking tray before lifting onto a wire rack.
   While the cookies are cooling, make the filling:
1. In a medium bowl, mix the confectioners' sugar and cinnamon together. Add the softened butter and mix well to a creamy consistency.
2. Grate the ginger, squeezing the juice into the mix, and stir well. If the mix becomes too liquid, add more confectioners' sugar until you have a thick consistency.

3. Refrigerate the mix for about 15 minutes. Spoon a small amount of the chilled mix (about the size of a quarter) onto the flat side of one cookie. Place another cookie over the top and gently squeeze them together to make a sandwich.

   Enjoy.

(Note: These baked cookies can go soft pretty quickly, especially on board. If you're not going to eat them immediately, cool the (unfilled) cookies and store them in an airtight container. You can also store the filling in an airtight container in the fridge for a week or more. Or you can do what we do, and just eat them immediately.)

Chapter 18

Still in Aruba!

During my week alone in Aruba waiting for Bob and Nic, I spent the majority of my time on the resort's private island, perfecting the art of becoming a professional beach bum. I became friends with the crew running the helicopter tour business at the end of the dock. I made friends with people that I met on the island, and I became familiar with a whole bunch of iguanas that gathered by the helicopter booking office, possibly hoping for a free ride. I started taking them lettuce every morning (the iguanas, not the helicopter staff). They were so tame they would climb onto my lap and eat out of my hands. Obviously, they were quite used to people feeding them. I had noticed that one of my neighbors on the dock also took them lettuce each morning.

By the end of the week, the iguanas would come running toward me as I approached the dock. I quickly became very fond of them and was able to identify some of them individually. Back on the boat, I was still surrounded by nature: Each morning two small finches would fly inside the main cabin and hop around looking for food. For once I was grateful that Nicho-San was back in Ohio, or it could have been bloody.

To discourage the finches from coming inside the boat, I started putting a little basket of food on deck. It worked like a charm, but then I found crumbs and tiny bird poops all over the cockpit and decks. And while I was eating, they would land on the table and want to share my food, which was very cute but not terribly hygienic, and I couldn't help thinking how much Bob would disapprove.

As the week went on, the finches became so tame they would land right next to me, showing no fear at all. I was also spending more time than I would have liked cleaning up their little poops all over the deck.

Thursday, July 23

Bob and Niki arrived today; I had cocktails and some delicious nibbles waiting for them. Once Niki had time to relax and get settled, Bob and I showed her around the resort, and I introduced her to the iguanas. Later she met the finches that she comically named Philippe and June. Soon another finch arrived, and Niki named that one Fernando. Word must have spread within the Aruban finch community that there were good eats to be had on the blue boat, because our daily visitors were gaining in numbers.

Every morning between 6 and 7 a.m., Niki and I would walk up to the hotel pool to swim—although when I say swim, I mean that I pretty much just splashed around while Niki swam forty laps. I had to admire her stamina. I did manage a pathetic ten laps, which included a quick coffee break halfway through.

We toured the shopping areas and seafront stalls in search of gifts for Niki to take back for her friends. I couldn't resist buying her a cute skirt from the designer shop Ralph Lauren. In another designer shop (that shall remain nameless), I decided against a really eye-catching pair of gold flip-flops when I saw the $680 price tag. I couldn't help wondering how on earth a tiny pair of flip-flops could cost that much—were they made of actual gold?

Later in the week we moved out of the harbor and took *Daisy* up along the coast toward Palm Beach to do some snorkeling. The water was very shallow, and there were so many shoals, we had to anchor about a mile off shore. The wind was really lovely so far out. It was a pleasant change from the sheltered, airless slip we had in the marina. We made the long, wet, and very choppy ride into shore in *Whoops-a-Daisy*, then walked up and down the beaches, stopping for a cocktail at one of the beach bars. The Palm Beach area beaches were teeming with people, and there was practically every type of watersport underway. It was a veritable hive of activity.

Aruba is ideal for water sports because the water here is absolutely perfect: calm, flat, and shallow. That explains why Aruba attracts tourists in the tens of thousands, which is great for the island's business but not what we were looking for. We decided to snorkel off the boat, instead of the beach, preferring the peace and quiet farther off shore.

Thursday, July 30

Edi arrived for a two-week visit. As small as the island is, there really is so much to see in Aruba, and I couldn't wait to explore it further with Edi. We rented a car—a slightly newer, luminous lime-green version of the yellow peril. It did, however, have great air-conditioning and a passenger handle that didn't come off when you tried to open the door. And unlike the yellow peril, it didn't squeak.

Bob, Niki, Edi, and I piled in and set off around the island, with me as the experienced guide, having recently gained extensive local knowledge following my two days in a car with Angie. We headed west toward the California Lighthouse, and I proudly pointed out the exclusive hotel where Angie and I had made our infamous escape. I told Bob to speed past the hotel while I ducked out of sight in the pretense of picking something up off the floor. I really hoped that the hotel staff wasn't still looking for the women who made off with free drinks from their bar. (I'm joking, of course!)

I was looking forward to taking Bob and Ed to La Trattoria el Faro Blanco restaurant, where Angie and I had eaten during our visit to the California Lighthouse. When we got to the restaurant, it was closed. So we headed back, this time following the road inland.

We drove around until we came to the natural bridge, another popular tourist attraction where you can expect to find busloads of tourists—and we did. There were the usual touristy gift shop, ice-cream bar, and cafe, but what was not so ordinary was a large sign on the premises that read No Farting in large, bold letters. It made me question the type of clientele they're accustomed to. I couldn't help but wonder what the penalty would be should you accidently, well, you know. Fortunately, none of us did, so I guess we'll never know. Anyway, back to more intellectual matters.

The natural bridge was one of Aruba's most popular attractions. The bridge was a formation of coral limestone, cut out by many years of pounding surf, and was one of the largest of these types of spans in the world. It stood 23 feet above sea level and spanned more than 100 feet. I say "stood" rather than "stands," because the bridge collapsed on September, 2, 2005. It fell down in the middle of the night (as so many things do), so no one was hurt. Just a stone's throw from the original bridge, nature was already busily carving out another natural bridge. We took a lot of photographs before getting back in the car and heading out again.

The new Natural Bridge.

Our next port of call was the Bushiribana Gold Mine, or rather the ruins of the gold mine. A rock heap and a crumbling stone wall are all that now remain of the Aruba Island Gold Mining Company. The views from the gold mine were spectacular and offered some wonderful photographic opportunities. All the mine buildings were constructed using a dry-wall technique, where rocks were fitted perfectly together without the use of mortar. Most of the original houses in Aruba—with their slanted roofs and tiny windows—were built using the dry-wall technique, which kept the dwellings cool inside by allowing the heat to rise. This technique is no longer in use today, but examples of these early structures can still be seen all over the island. We climbed through the ruins, taking photographs as we went.

The Aruban economy was boosted by the discovery of gold in 1824, when a young boy found a couple of nuggets in the dry valleys on the northeast coast. The area eventually yielded 3,000 pounds of gold for the island.

From the gold mine, we headed to the caves, which will fascinate anyone with an interest in ancient history, cave exploration, or nature. All three caves are located within close proximity to one another on the southeastern side of Aruba: Guadirikiri, Huliba, and Fontein.

Guadirikiri Cave stretches for approximately 150 meters (492 feet) and is famous for its two natural chambers, illuminated by sunlight that comes streaming through the holes in the cave's ceiling. We climbed stairs and passed through two dark corridors to reach the large open cavern. We got some amazing photographs, despite my close calls dropping my camera in the dark. The beams of light in the large opening of the cave's center were spectacular; the temperature was very cool, almost cold, and it was so silent you could hear a pin drop. This was possibly the easiest cave to navigate, although a flashlight would definitely have made our exploration easier (and safer).

Huliba Cave, also known as the Baranca Sunu (Naked Rock) Cave, is more commonly known as "the tunnel of love." A fascinating ancient folk story about this cave tells of a native tribal chief's daughter who fell in love with a man the chief disapproved of. The daughter refused to give up her paramour, so the chief had them both sealed in the cave to die. After death, their rebellious spirits smashed through the cave's roof and soared toward the heavens, defying the tribal chief's wishes by remaining together even in death. The holes in the roof of the cave where the planks of sunlight stream through are said to be where the two lovers' souls escaped. The tunnel of love is advertised throughout Aruba as a "romantic tourist attraction." I'm afraid I would beg to differ; in reality the cave is overrun with cockroaches, which quickly became evident when I stood still for more than a few seconds. The cave is dark, damp, and horribly claustrophobic. As we navigated the dark recesses of the cave, the bats startled and scared the pants off us. Although they're quite harmless, they scared us by flying close to us. The stagnant air and bat droppings do not a romantic place make. My hair stands on end at the thought of two people trapped until death in this cave. Huliba Cave is *not* on my not-to-be missed list. Aruba has many other wonderful tourist attractions; I'm afraid my personal choice would be to forget this one.

The last cave we explored was Fontein Cave near Boca Prins, which has earned the reputation of being the most interesting of all the caves in Aruba because of its original Indian drawings on the ceilings. However, Fontein Cave is also the home of the long-tongued bat.

Niki, Edi, and I found the caves fascinating, but Bob wasn't keen to venture in. Exploration of the caves involved having to almost crawl at times, and the farther we went in, the more intense the heat became. So Bob waited outside while Niki, Edi, and I bravely followed our guide through.

The guide pointed out paintings from some of the island's original inhabitants. Unfortunately, a few previous visitors displayed their ignorance to the world by defacing parts of the caves with graffiti, which had made it necessary for guards and gates to ensure the continued protection of the caves and their drawings.

From Fontein Cave we drove through the Arikok National Park. The park had recently been reopened, with new roads and proper drainage to cope with the runoff from the unexpected rainfall. Rocky outcrops between the formations in Aruba have created microclimatic conditions that support the flora and fauna here. There are a few different varieties of wildlife, some indigenous to the island, such as the cascabel (Aruba's rattlesnake), which is the only venomous snake on the island. This protected snake now has fewer than 500 of its species left on the island, due to its decreasing habitat.

The santanero, Aruba's cat-eyed snake, is another that is unique to this island, as are the kododo blauw, whiptail lizard, and two bird species: the shoco, a burrowing owl, and the prikichi, a parakeet found only in the ABC islands.

From the park, we continued south to San Nicolas. We hadn't eaten, and I was getting grumpy and quite desperate to locate a restaurant. As we drove farther south, nothing we passed was open, other than the occasional gas station. I was starting to wonder if people ate lunch in Aruba. We were all feeling quite miserable from hunger when we accidentally drove past the Flying Fishbone, a restaurant that Angie and I had searched and searched for the previous week without success. This restaurant had a wonderful reputation on the island, particularly for its fabulous fresh fish. We parked the car and walked in, but to our dismay it was closed; apparently they only served dinner.

A couple of guys were there cleaning, so we asked if we could look around. The Flying Fishbone was a truly delightful restaurant that literally spills out onto the beach. The tables on the beach go right down to the shore, and each table has a shoe rack so you could store your shoes and wiggle your toes in the sand and the surf as you eat. We immediately decided that this was where we wanted to eat dinner. We glanced over a menu to find that the food was definitely not cheap, but the offerings sounded adventurous and inventive. We reserved a table for 5:30 p.m., which couldn't come soon enough: we hadn't eaten for almost eight hours.

Still starving and miserable but optimistic at the thought of a wonderful dinner in three hours, we headed out again. We eventually arrived at San Nicolas and parked on the beach where we found a little shack serving food—a welcome sight. I was so hungry I would have eaten anything. The beach is beautiful, and the water clean, clear, and turquoise with gently rolling waves. Unfortunately, the island's oil refinery rather overshadows the beach here, which is such a shame because it would be truly magnificent otherwise.

The New Jersey-based oil company, Lago, established the oil refinery in San Nicolas in 1924, bringing real prosperity to the island of Aruba. Unemployment dropped and the island flourished. Unfortunately, as world demand for oil decreased in the late 1970s and early 1980s, the refinery was forced to close in 1985. In 1991, the refinery was reopened by another company, Coastal El Paso Corporation, but was sold again in 2004 to the Valero Oil Corporation, the main distributor on the island.

Everyone enjoyed the beach lunch of shrimp and fries, which was just enough to keep us going until dinner.

Dinner on the beach at the Flying Fishbone lived up to its reputation. Our table wasn't quite on the edge of the shore: we noticed that those particular tables were reserved for two (usually honeymooners).

We wiggled our toes in the cool sand as we ate. It was one of the loveliest meals I've shared with my family; had Danni been with us, it would have been perfect. The food was good, the service friendly, and the setting breathtaking. This restaurant is another on my not-to-be-missed list, if not for the food than absolutely for the atmosphere and friendly service.

For the rest of Niki's stay, we swam at 6 a.m. every morning, shopped at all the local stores, relaxed on the topless beach, hand-fed the flamingos, worked out at the island gym, tested cocktails at the local bars, and generally had a relaxing, fun time.

One afternoon at the beach, we were packing up and getting ready to return to *Daisy* when Niki pointed to the water and called out, "Look, a shark!" I spotted the fin above the water and watched the shark swim slowly toward the bridge. But as the rest of the people on the beach started running toward Niki to see where she was pointing, the shark swam away.

Everyone stood watching and waiting to see if the shark would come back, but it never did. Niki swore it was a lemon shark; she said she recognized it from the ones she had seen on the Discovery Channel. Later, on the way back to the marina, I asked the boat captain whether he had ever seen sharks at the resort. "Oh, yes," he responded with enthusiasm, sporting a wide grin. "We get lemon sharks here all the time, but they're harmless, so you needn't worry." I noticed a glint in his eye as he said it, which led me to suspect otherwise!

Every day after that, we looked for the shark, but we never saw him again. The next afternoon Niki found a large living conch, definitely not the most attractive of the ocean's creatures. In fact, I wouldn't hesitate in saying it was really quite ugly. The poor thing was like a gigantic brown slimy garden snail. I don't think I'll ever eat conch again. We put it carefully back in the water, hoping it would work its way out to sea instead of ending up on someone's dinner plate.

Niki and I are very similar in our fascination with little creatures. She showed me dozens of beautiful tiny sea stars and brittle stars found under pebbles and shells in the shallow water, as well as countless hermit crabs back on the beach. We found a few more beautiful shells (uninhabited, of course) for my collection. The two of us had endless fun. It didn't take much to entertain us, particularly on a beach as lovely as this one. The only downside to this little island was its close proximity to the airport: it got a little noisy when the planes flew low overhead. In fact, the planes flew so low that the little boats that transport you from the harbor to the island had to stop and wait while the planes approached the runway before they continued on again.

Sunday, August 9

Niki flew home to Atlanta. Bob and I drove her to the airport and said a very tearful good-bye. Edi moved into the double guest room, while I prepared the bunks for Danni and Julie, who were due to arrive in two days. My little floating hotel was fully booked for the month.

The first time anyone visits *Daisy*, I stress the importance of bringing a soft-sided suitcase: People who have never taken a yachting vacation have absolutely no idea of the limited storage space on board, even on a boat as big as *Daisy*. So with that in mind, I e-mailed ahead to Danni's friend Julie and explained as clearly as I could that guests must bring only soft-sided collapsible bags and a minimum of clothing: Bathing suits, shorts, T-shirts, one nice dress or pants in case we eat at a posh restaurant, one pair of shoes, one pair of sandals, and flip-flops are all that are required.

My request obviously fell on deaf ears, or maybe Julie just overlooked the e-mails. Oh boy, was I ever unprepared for Julie!

Let me explain quickly: Julie is a beautiful, petite fitness instructor who is always immaculate, even in workout gear—a tiny little thing that would take up no space at all, or so I thought.

Mango Marinated Seared Tuna with Tropical Fruit Salsa

Salsa:
2 mangos, diced
1 medium pineapple, diced
1 large papaya, diced
1 large red bell pepper, roasted and diced
1 bunch cilantro, chopped
Juice from 2 limes
4 jalapenos, minced
4 scallions, finely chopped

Marinade:
¼ cup mango juice
3 tablespoons canola oil plus 2 more tablespoons for cooking
2 tablespoons balsamic vinegar
1 teaspoon ground nutmeg
1-inch piece fresh ginger, peeled and finely chopped
¼ teaspoon crushed red pepper flakes
Salt and freshly ground black pepper
6 tuna steaks, about 4 to 6 ounces each

1. Mix the salsa ingredients together in a small bowl; cover and refrigerate.
2. In a small bowl, whisk together the marinade ingredients; pour into a large plastic zip bag. Add the tuna steaks. Seal and shake the bag to evenly distribute the marinade and cover the fish. Put the bag in the refrigerator and marinate for at least 1 hour, turning occasionally.
3. Heat the oil in a large skillet over medium heat. Remove the tuna from the marinade, pat dry, and cook until done, about 3 to 4 minutes per side. (Adjust the cooking time, depending upon the thickness of the steaks and how well done you like your tuna.)
    Top with salsa and serve.
    Enjoy.

Chapter 19

More Aruba

Tuesday, August 10

I was out on the dock feeding my little troop of iguana friends, when out the corner of my eye I glimpsed this huge black object being pushed along the dock toward me. Barely visible behind the large black wheelie object were two heads, Danni's and Julie's. Bob followed some way behind, looking less than amused.

"Hi!" I said running toward them excitely to give hugs and kisses. "What's this? Did you bring your own boat?" I laughed, really hoping that they were pushing the gigantic suitcase as an act of kindness for a family of twelve who were on their way to the cruise ship.

"No," Danni said, raising one eyebrow and smiling at me. "This is Julie's suitcase." Bob shot me one of those wide-eyed looks that said, "*Seriously, I mean seriously . . .*"

I stared open mouthed at the enormous hard-sided suitcase. Was she serious? And more importantly, where the bloody hell were we going to put it? I glanced across the bay to the enormous cruise ship on the dock and couldn't help thinking that even they would have a hard time wheeling this case on board, let alone us trying to get it across the narrow passarella to board *Daisy*. I looked at Julie and realized Danni wasn't kidding. "I'm so, so sorry," Julie said, looking genuinely embarrassed. "I tried to pack light!" I wanted to say, "You failed

201

miserably," but instead I replied, rather unconvincingly, "Um, OK, well I'm sure we'll find somewhere for it." Julie's suitcase was so large, I was certain we would probably just end up towing it like another dinghy behind the boat.

In the end, she had to unpack its contents up on the dock. Watching her unpack, I realized that she had obviously either overlooked or ignored my e-mail: there were about fifty different outfits and at least twenty-five pairs of shoes. We managed to wedge the half-empty case into the boson's locker, which, as luck would have it, had some space available because all the fenders that were usually stored there were currently tied alongside. I made a mental note to call instead of write to my future visitors to make sure they absolutely understood the packing instructions.

As soon as Julie and Danni had finished unpacking (many hours later), I served cocktails and hors d'oeuvres on deck, then we all headed over to the little island to snorkel. Later, I served cocktails and dinner on board: At least with Julie here I had a chance to drag a few of my nice dresses out of the mothballs and try and look smart for a change.

Wednesday, August 11

In the morning while Edi was sitting up on deck, a lady approached *Daisy* and asked Edi whether he would consider letting her use *Daisy* for a fashion photo shoot. Edi explained that he would have to clear it with the captain, and if she could come back later, he could give her a reply. We all thought that sounded like fun, so after discussing the rules (no shoes, no smoking, etc.), we agreed to let them perform the shoot. Bob insisted that Edi take charge and keep an eye on things. The arrangements were made, and we agreed they could perform the shoot the following morning.

That afternoon Danni filmed Julie's "Daily Motivational Challenge," a ten-minute exercise program, right there on the end of the dock overlooking the ocean. Julie does this every day in her tireless effort to motivate people to get fit and maintain a healthier lifestyle. (You can watch it on YouTube; just search Julie Wilkes.)

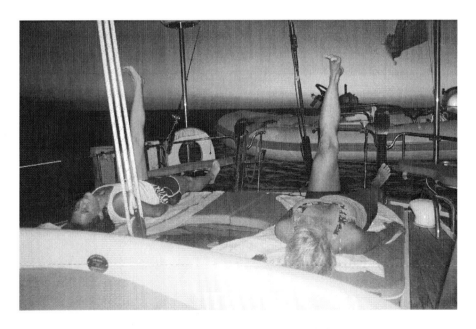

Danni and Julie working out on deck.

Danni, Julie, and Edi went over to the island gym for a late afternoon work-out. I admire my children's commitment to fitness, whereas I am convinced that living aboard is enough exercise for me. Bob and I did go snorkeling for about an hour, which was quite enough exercise as far as I was concerned. The lovely afternoon on the beach was followed by a lazy evening on board, playing Mexican Train and drinking cocktails.

Thursday, August 12

The fashion shoot troupe arrived midmorning. The entourage included a hairdresser, a make-up artist, a make-up artist's assistant, a photographer, a photographer's assistant, a fashion director, a director's assistant, models, a magazine representative, a wardrobe assistant, and the list just goes on. Edi and I turned on the air-con below decks as everyone arrived. Fabulous clothes were hung in the saloon, two gorgeous models (one male, one female) boarded, and Edi and I stood back and watched while the shoot took place. The heat was really intense, so we made pitcher after pitcher of ice water for everybody.

Bob, Danni, and Julie went over to the island to get out of the way for the shoot, while Edi and I stayed on board. It was fascinating to watch the proceedings and all the work involved with getting a photograph just right. Bob, Danni, and Julie returned after lunch, and the shoot was still in full swing. We all kept a low profile and tried not to interfere with their work. But when the shoot was complete, we all reached for our cameras to enjoy our own photo opportunity with the models and crew. When the troupe cleared out, we freshened up for a dinner out on the town, Bob's treat.

Friday August 13, through Sunday, August 16

We spent Edi's last vacation days visiting the island, sunbathing, swimming, working out at the gym, and just enjoying everything Aruba had to offer. After we dropped Edi off at the airport, we left the harbor and sailed around the island to snorkel off shore. The sea breezes felt so lovely after the airless confines of the harbor. We decided to stay overnight on our anchorage—a decision I would later regret.

That night while *Daisy* rocked gently on the water, I was deep in a blissfully peaceful sleep when I was startled awake by a blinding light that poured through the bedroom portholes. It was so bright, I thought the aliens had landed. I screamed, "Bob!" and he jumped up, disorientated and confused. The two of us frantically scrambled around for our clothes while the blinding light continued to focus on us. I grabbed the sheets in an attempt to cover myself. Bob pulled on a pair of shorts and ran up on deck. I could hear the low rumble of boat engines. My imagination started spinning at Olympic speed on its wheel of impending disasters. It took my worst fears to totally new levels, and my immediate, rather more rational but nonetheless scary thought was, "Oh crap, pirates!" When I heard voices, my next thought was, "OMG, they're going to rob and murder us." My mind raced back to the books I'd read on piracy on the high seas. What to do? If only the craziness that is my imagination would simply slow down, just for a second, I could think. The light had shifted away from the bedroom up to the cockpit, and I could see the shadow of the boat alongside us. Peering through the porthole, I could just make out the shadows of about five men—all armed, heavily armed. At this point I almost fainted; my imagination had keeled over and was lying comatose with her legs in the air. I could still hear the men talking to Bob. I was frozen to the spot. I thought about grabbing my chef's knife, but what good would that do? There were at least five of them. Then with horror I remembered the girls in the front cabins. If the pirates found them, they would kidnap the girls for sure. My mind flooded with of all the kidnappings I had heard and read about recently, including my cousin's friend and her husband, who had been kidnapped off their boat and were being held for ransom. It took a few minutes for my eyes to adjust from the blinding light and my little brain to control the panic and decide upon the best course of action. The conversation on deck continued, but I couldn't work out what was being said. Then abruptly the boat engines revved up, and the boat took off, leaving *Daisy* bouncing around in the wake. I sat paralyzed in fear. My heart was pounding so hard, I thought it would jump up through my mouth. What was happening? Did the pirates kidnap Bob? How would I get the boat back to the marina? How would I find him? Were any of them aboard? How could I protect the girls? What would they do with us? So many crazy, impossible scenarios wracked my brain, I thought I would pass out. But I couldn't pass out, or they would just throw me overboard. My always-too-active imagination had woken up from her coma and was doing backflips and tearing her hair out.

After what seemed like hours but was probably only a couple of minutes, Bob came back to the bedroom and casually announced "coast guard." I almost fainted with relief, but then I looked at the clock: 2:30 a.m. "What the hell!" I yelled. "It's 2:30 in the bloody morning!" I was not amused; anger immediately took over from fear and the immense relief that Bob was OK. They had scared the living daylights out of me.

"They were just checking on what we're doing out here. We're anchored about a mile off shore; it probably does look suspicious," Bob said, shrugging his shoulders, as if it was no big deal. But I was furious. Why couldn't they have checked on us during daylight, or at least at a slightly more civilized hour? I was still fuming about their shining that spotlight through our bedroom window and giving me a near coronary.

Apparently our experience was not an unusual one, as most yachties who have made the mistake of anchoring off one of Aruba's beaches will tell you.

The coast guard around Aruba is very, very strict and particularly vigilant in their efforts to keep drugs off the island. Thankfully, Julie and Danni had slept through the visit. I think they would have been scared to death had they seen five armed men alongside *Daisy* in the middle of the night—although that wasn't the only reason I was glad that Danni and Julie had stayed out of view. Had the men caught sight of our two gorgeous guests, heaven only knows what could have happened. I've read and heard many scary stories of corrupt officials; you never really know. My fears were, in fact, not as irrational as one might think: there are more and more boat attacks, shootings, and kidnappings every day throughout the Caribbean. It's a fear I live with daily while on board.

Monday, August 17

On Julie's last day with us, we didn't want to waste any time, so we rented a car and once again took off around the island. We drove out to the California Lighthouse and to the caves. We took some amazing photographs inside the caves. It was a fun day with a lot of other interesting stops along the way. Danni seemed very sad at the thought of Julie leaving. But I suspect she may have been a little sadder at the thought of being left alone with Mum and Dad for another week.

Danni at the gold mine.

Danni and Julie, a right chocolaty mess, even fitness guru's eat chocolate

Danni and Julie with resident beach flamingo!

Tuesday, August 25

The time flew by, and before I knew it, it was time for Danni to fly home. I'm always sad when our guests leave, especially when it's one of our children.

The morning was spent getting the boat ready for the sail back to Curacao, before our (or rather my) emotional, tearful good-byes. Bob drove Danni to the airport, and the minute he returned we cast off, setting sail for Curacao.

The return trip was by far my worst experience on *Daisy*. The long leg back to Curacao was about as rough as it could be, into the wind and current with huge swells and gusting wind. I was like a dying duck in a thunderstorm, cowering under the dodger, desperately trying but failing miserably to stay dry. I spent the majority of the leg hanging limply over the side, vomiting for England.

I couldn't wait to get off *Daisy* and back onto dry land. I didn't think I would ever want to get back on a boat again.

Funny how short a bad memory can be. By the time we brought *Daisy* alongside at the Curacao boatyard, I was already mentally planning the next trip. I can't help but wonder how foolhardy this makes me.

[Cook's note]

Quite often in the islands, I've found English cider in the supermarkets, and when I do, I just can't resist making this typical English dish. Talk about comfort food.

Chicken with Somerset Cider

1 tablespoon olive oil
6 chicken breasts (with the skin on)
Sea salt and freshly ground black pepper
2 tablespoons unsalted butter
1 medium red onion, diced
3 tablespoons all-purpose flour
1¼ cups chicken stock (preferably homemade)
1 tablespoon whole-grain mustard
1 teaspoon Italian mixed herbs
¼ teaspoon freshly grated nutmeg
2 apples, peeled and chopped (I like Russets, but Granny Smiths are good, too)
8 ounces wild mushrooms, cleaned and sliced
2 cups cider (plus a glass to drink while you're cooking)
2 cups heavy cream
2 cups cheddar cheese, grated
1. Preheat the oven to 400 degrees F.

1. Heat the olive oil in a large sauté pan over medium-high heat.
2. Season the chicken breasts well with salt and pepper, and sear the chicken in the pan until golden on both sides.
3. Remove the chicken breasts from the pan and place them into a deep ovenproof dish in the preheated oven to continue cooking for about 30 minutes.
4. Add the butter to the same sauté pan used for cooking the chicken. When the butter has melted and stopped sizzling, add the onions. Stirring gently, cook the onions until soft and transparent.
5. Slowly add the flour, one tablespoon at a time, stirring constantly.
6. Add the chicken stock very slowly, stirring well to incorporate all the flour without making lumps. Stir in the whole-grain mustard.

7. Add the Italian mixed herbs, nutmeg, apples, and mushrooms to the pan and continue cooking for about 5 to 8 minutes.
8. Slowly add the cider, followed by the cream. Stir well to mix. Cook for another 8 to 10 minutes to reduce the liquid. Season with salt and pepper.
9. Remove the chicken from the oven, pour the sauce over the chicken, top with the grated cheddar cheese, and pop under a hot grill (broil) until the cheese is golden and bubbling. Serve immediately with creamy mashed potatoes.

    Enjoy.

[Cook's note]

I decided to save the best for last: my Daisy Shake. This is my kicked-up-a-couple-of-notches chocolate shake with a twist or two. It's loaded with calories—so beware. I serve it in a martini glass instead of the usual milk shake tumbler.

Daisy Shake

2 cups of good-quality chocolate milk
¼ cup organic creamy peanut butter
¼ cup Nutella
1 cup rich dark-chocolate ice cream
¼ cup Baileys liqueur
Splash of cognac
Whipped cream, for garnish
Put all the ingredients (except the whipped cream) into a blender and buzz till thoroughly mixed.
Serve immediately in martini glasses with a dollop of whipped cream on top.
Enjoy.

Chapter 20

Six Months Later—Back in St. Maarten

Simpson Bay Lagoon, St. Maarten

Coordinates: 18 04'N 63 03'W

Wednesday, April 21, 2010

After a wonderful almost-six-month break on land with Danni and Edi, in March I returned to the boat in sunny St. Maarten. I had been keeping myself very busy with all sorts of delightful jobs, such as sanding and varnishing the floorboards, the toe-rail, and the cockpit table; scrubbing and cleaning the teak decks; washing cushions; and polishing all the stainless steel. I had scrubbed and polished *Whoops-a-Daisy*'s bottom until you could see your face in it. What a claim to fame, I had to laugh at myself: "bottom scrubber and polisher"! Hmmm, I wonder what my mum would say about that?

Captain Bob arrived on Tuesday, after working for a few weeks back on the mainland, and we were both looking forward to getting out of the marina and having some fun. We were planning to visit St. Barts, in particular Columbia Bay.

The next morning, with a busy day ahead of us, we were up before daylight. We set about getting the boat tidy and secure, ready for our sail over to St. Barts. Getting the boat ready for sail is one of those jobs that I hate because everything, and I mean everything, has to be stowed. I'm always trying to make *Daisy* feel like a home by having stuff about: a vase of flowers, baskets of shells, books and art materials everywhere, and more kitchen equipment than many restaurants have (something that drives Bob crazy—but what can I tell you, I love to cook). I am, in truth, a bit of a hoarder—or as I prefer to call it, a "collector." To Captain Bob, it's all just "stuff," stuff he would rather not have on his otherwise tidy and organized boat. I admit that, without all my stuff, getting ready to sail would be a great deal easier and quicker, but I like having it around, so I have to deal with stowing it each time we set sail. And because I had been living on the boat alone for a few weeks, I had a lot of stuff about everywhere.

At 8:30 a.m., I took Bob in *Whoops-a-Daisy* to the customs office to check out. While he was there, I did some last-minute provisioning at the Garden Market. I collected him an hour later, and we headed back to *Daisy*. There were still a couple of jobs to do before we could set sail, and fortunately (or should I say *unusually*), we didn't encounter any difficulties or disasters during our preparations for leaving. By midday we were stowed, tidy, and underway.

The weather was beautiful to the south, and the seas wonderfully calm. We had perfect 12 to 14 knots of wind and were able to raise the sails and enjoy a very pleasant sail, eating lunch en route. We zigzagged a bit during the crossing to keep our speed up, and, at one point, we came very close to another yacht. You would think that, out there on the ocean with all the miles and miles of space around you, it would be easy to avoid one other boat. But no, we managed to come within inches of colliding. The remainder of the journey was enjoyed without any other unfortunate incidents (well, at least once I'd recovered from my near panic attack over our close call with the other yacht).

Bob put out the fishing line and caught a small tuna. I became quite tearful as I poured vodka into its gills: It really upset me to have to kill a living creature, but I had to do it, otherwise I would have felt like a hypocrite. I'm happy to eat fish, so I should be prepared to kill them, right? At least that's how I look at it. Bob gutted the fish, and then I cleaned it. I wrapped it well and packed it in ice for later.

Arriving at St. Barts, we picked up a mooring in Columbia Bay quite close to shore and spotted turtles in every direction. We immediately put on our swimwear and went snorkeling. Within minutes we spotted several turtles feeding on the grassy beds beneath us. We also spotted a couple of stingrays. Columbia Bay is the best bay to easily spot turtles and stingrays; the grassy seabed provides the perfect feeding ground for them.

Late afternoon, the peace and quiet of the bay was suddenly shattered by a couple of kids from one of the megayachts anchored outside the bay. They came speeding into the bay on their Jet Skis, acting like complete morons: circling the yachts anchored in the bay, making wakes, driving at ridiculously high speeds, and doing doughnuts. (This is against regulations in a marine park, as anyone with an ounce of intelligence knows.) Fortunately, someone (not us, although I would have liked to) obviously reported them, because within minutes the authorities arrived and dragged the kids and their Jet Skis out of the bay, as everyone in the bay stood on their yachts watching. Once peace was restored, we relaxed on deck with a couple of cocktails and watched the sunset.

For dinner I cooked the tuna with sautéed peppers, mushrooms, and baby carrots, followed by crème brûlée for dessert. We spent a lovely evening on deck, listening to music and watching the stars. This had been such a wonderful day, the kind of day dreams are made of, with no disasters, no breakages—in fact, no problems at all.

It was another beautiful Caribbean morning. I sat up on deck dropping breadcrumbs over the side to feed the growing shoal of remoras under the boat, when I suddenly spotted what appeared to be a large reef shark circling below them. I called out to Bob, but by the time he came up on deck, the shark had disappeared. I continued feeding the remoras. There were at least six or seven of them now, as well as a couple of other large fish and a shoal of smaller ones—all of them frantically splashing about in a feeding frenzy.

After breakfast we took *Whoops-a-Daisy* all the way around to Gustavia, which was a 20-minute extremely choppy ride. One gets quite a workout when traveling in a dinghy at warp speed on rough water. And when Bob drives, he has only two speeds: full throttle and stop. At full throttle, I'm literally thrown up in the air over every wave. Sometimes it's fun, but this was a bit too rough for me. We tied up alongside, and Bob saw to customs and immigration while I shopped for a few provisions and stopped for a delicious coffee at Le Bar de L'Oubli.

Bob joined me at the bar for a cappuccino and a croissant before we headed out around town to do some window-shopping. St. Barts is absolutely beautiful but also very expensive, so our shopping was more about looking rather than actually buying. Our extravagant expense was some new earplugs for Bob at the local dive store.

We arrived back at *Daisy* midmorning to go snorkeling again with the turtles and stingrays. While I prepared lunch, Bob was diving under the boat cleaning the hull. I suddenly heard him call out, so I rushed up on deck to find him bleeding from one ear. He didn't have any pain or discomfort and thought it was possibly due to the new earplugs. But he got out of the water, because in these waters one really doesn't want to be bleeding (blood in the water attracts sharks). We decided it was best to stay out of the water for a couple of days, which was such a shame because we came to this bay specifically for the snorkeling. Oh well, we had already enjoyed two great snorkeling sessions, so we spent a quiet afternoon and evening relaxing on deck and reading.

Late afternoon, a megayacht pulled into the bay and proceeded to play really loud music while a bunch of young girls sang and danced on the top deck. As the evening wore on, the music got louder and the singing made me want to stuff cotton wool in my ears. It continued into the early hours, making sleep impossible. I wonder sometimes about people who behave that way. Don't they realize that the people on the other boats in the bay may not wish to listen to their raucous behavior? Edi is always joking about wanting to have cannons on board *Daisy*, and at that time I really wished we had. Oh, just the thought of firing a cannonball at the noisy megayacht made me giggle. It certainly would have brought a rude and abrupt halt to their drunken noise fest.

Friday, April 23, 2010

After a somewhat restless night, I was woken by the most glorious sunrise. Planks of brilliant golden light stole through the cracks in the curtains, shooting across the bedroom and landing on my face, blinding me with their brilliance. Up on deck, the sky was a painter's palette of warm, glowing colors, from the palest yellow deepening to the darkest crimson. Rays of gold lit the water in the bay, which was as still and clear as glass, and I could see straight to the bottom. The beauty of mornings like this is impossible to accurately describe (please excuse my clumsy attempts to do so). I fetched a little bread from the galley to feed the remoras under the boat. There were at least eight of them this morning—my little group was growing. The megayacht that had been so noisy through the night had pulled out of the bay early in the morning. For them, the bay had obviously been just an overnight party stop.

After breakfast Bob and I decided it was too perfect of a morning to miss: we absolutely had to go snorkeling. I packed and covered his ear with cotton wool and waterproof bandages as best I could, and in we went. We swam over to the rocky shore where we saw the beautiful angelfish again, a colorful trigger-fish, one of the largest cowfish I'd ever seen, as well as many other fabulous and colorful species. We swam back out over the grass beds to watch the turtles and rays. When it was time to return to *Daisy*, we noticed a couple of large shadows lurking on the seabed directly under her. On closer inspection, the shadows turned out to be two rather large (quite a bit bigger than us) nurse sharks. We quietly floated on the surface above them for a few minutes while Bob photo-graphed them.

You may wonder why Bob and I hovered so close to the sharks. Nurse sharks are known to be sluggish during the day, keeping the majority of their activity between the hours of dusk till dawn when they're actively feeding. Common in tropical waters over inshore coral reefs, nurse sharks are the most frequently spotted sharks by divers and snorkelers in the Caribbean. They're usually harm-less unless provoked, but I have to say this statement confuses me: I'm quite interested in knowing exactly how one defines "provoked." Obviously, I'm not going to swim up and poke them with a sharp stick, but could swimming around them while they're sleeping be considered provoking? I decided that it was prob-ably best to simply keep a safe distance.

Later in the afternoon, a couple from another Oyster in the bay introduced themselves, and we invited them on board for a drink and a chat. One aspect of boat life that I really love was just how friendly boat people are, especially the yachties.

As soon as our guests left, I immediately popped back in the water to watch the sharks, which were still sleeping peacefully in *Daisy*'s shadow. I swam quietly above them, fascinated and amazed that I wasn't nervous being this close to them. I was floating almost motionless on the surface, watching and taking photographs, when Bob called for me to swim back closer to the boat. I had drifted quite a ways. My movement must have disturbed the sharks, be-cause as I swam back to the boat, both sharks moved off the bottom and started swimming toward me. It's funny how fast one can get out of the water when motivated, even while wearing flippers. Wonder Woman, look out: I could ap-parently move at the speed of light, too. It turned out the sharks moved only about ten feet before settling down for another rest, but I had watched them for long enough: this was not a good time to discover the meaning of the word "provoke"!

After lunch I was back in the water again. The sharks had moved on, and there were two beautiful stingrays in their place. And the remoras under *Daisy* had grown in number to ten. A turtle swam very close to me, stopping to peer into my mask. He tilted his head from side to side and locked eyes with me. I could have reached out and touched him, but I'd seen how sharp their teeth are, so I kept my arms and fingers close by my side. The turtle stared for a while then circled around me before surfacing for air and descending again to the grassy beds below. I obviously held little interest for him.

I spent the rest of the afternoon relaxing on deck while Bob completed unfinished jobs on board, like fixing the broken navigation light and jiggery TV lift. It was a very, very hot day, and I knew I had burnt my back again with all the snorkeling.

We waited until 5 p.m. when the sun was low in the sky and the temperature was a little cooler to take the dinghy ashore for a predinner beach walk and quick swim before returning to *Daisy* for our ritual cocktail at sunset.

As it happened, I had gotten a little carried away with my snorkeling during the day, because my bum was a brilliant crimson, like a baboon's; I'm sure it would glow in the dark. It also had all the heat that goes along with bad sunburn—adding a whole new meaning to the term "hot seat"!

My plans for serving the leftover tuna for dinner were not so successful. We had eaten the tuna for lunch and dinner the night before, and one can only eat so much tuna. I ended up feeding it to the remoras. So I made us an omelet instead. I was too tired to watch a movie and fell asleep right after dinner. I really must be getting old.

St. Barts to St. Eustatius
Coordinates: St. Barts 17 54' 16"N, 062 50'38"W, St. Eustatius 11 38' 31"N, 63 09'72"W

Saturday, April 24

The minute we finished breakfast, we cast off and motored around the head to Gustavia, where we dropped anchor. Bob went ashore and cleared us out with customs.

We weighed anchor for St. Eustatius shortly before noon. It was a lovely clear day, but there was absolutely no wind. I thought the doldrums must had left the Pacific and arrived in the Caribbean. We motored for about half of the leg. As a little wind picked up, we raised the sails and enjoyed a very peaceful 3- to 4-knot sail across, eating lunch along the way. I know this doesn't sound very exciting, but I loved it when there was only a little wind; it was so gentle, peaceful, and quiet, and I wasn't seasick or scared half out my wits. If only sailing were always like this, it wouldn't be a problem for me (and my hamster—that is, my vivid imagination—could retire), although Bob would probably die of boredom.

As we approached St. Eustatius, we spotted several tankers and large cargo ships anchored off the island. We pulled into Gallows Bay to find a good spot to drop anchor. We arrived too early in the year to see the flamboyant trees in bloom. From the shore right up to the top of the cliff, there are usually bright red, green, and yellow splashes of color—a brilliant floral display like something from a Vincent van Gogh painting.

The bay was a little rolly; it usually is here, although it has to be said the pale aquamarine water that deepened to a dark peacock blue was crystal clear, with visibility straight to the seabed. Bob took the dinghy over to the customs building at 4:45 p.m., only to discover that they were closed. The customs office was advertised as being open till 5 p.m., but as so often is the case in the Caribbean, they had all gone home early. Typical, laid-back island life.

For dinner I cooked a delicious sea bass, a vast improvement over the previous night's tuna disaster. After dinner I just couldn't sit through Bob's rubbishy movie choice, so I went into the guest room and watched *Julie and Julia* again. Our plan for the next day was to hike up the Quill, St. Eustatius's dormant volcano; it's something we've always threatened to do, and I really hoped the climb wasn't going to finish me off.

Sunday, April 25, 2010

We were up early to head over to the customs office. We left *Whoops-a-Daisy* tied to the dock, and, having finally cleared in with customs, we took a cab on a very brief sightseeing tour of the island, which took all of five minutes. The cab driver dropped us at the foot of the hiking trail to the Quill. As I looked up to the rim of the crater, I couldn't help but ask myself once again, "Why exactly am I doing this?"

"Which way?"

We set off, armed with cans of mosquito spray and other motorized deterrents clipped to our belts, bottles of iced water, suntan lotion, and a change of clothes for me for when I got all sweaty. The trail up the Quill actually zigzagged very gently up the side of the volcano with only a few steep paths, but in the tremendous heat, I found the hike quite exhausting. My heavy backpack was sticking to my back and getting heavier by the minute, rivers of sweat were running into my eyes, and my legs were starting to seriously wobble and ache. Danni and Edi would have run all the way up without even breaking a sweat. I felt quite pathetic.

Breathless, sweaty, slightly irritable, and much more achy than I should have been at my age, we arrived at the crater rim and took in the incredible beauty of the rain forest growing within the crater.

The climb to the rim was supposed to take forty-five to sixty minutes, but for yours truly it took longer. I had to keep stopping: I was breathing so heavily, I thought I was going to pass out. I removed my backpack and sat on a rock just to take the weight off my feet for a moment. I'd gone about as far as I could go, but Bob was determined to see more and continued on alone, descending into the rain forest within the crater. The explorer in him was alive and kicking. I waited breathlessly with the company of a very friendly rooster that didn't leave my side until Bob returned. I wondered what a rooster was doing all the way up here at the top of a volcano. He was probably waiting for me to keel over so he could chew on my bones. Thinking about my experience, I would imagine quite a few people expire after the trek up. It wasn't a very comforting thought, and I was anxious for Bob's return. I only had to wait about twenty minutes before he came bursting back through the bushes like David Bellamy (a well-known British botanist), with leaves stuck in his hair, a big stick in his hand, and a ridiculous grin on his face.

Bob and the Rooster!

Sadly for me, he wasn't finished yet; exhilarated by his trek into the rain forest, Bob then decided to climb even higher to the other side of the crater rim, about another 100 feet. I had to wonder where he got his stamina. The rooster settled down comfortably by my side, patiently waiting. Bob returned about thirty minutes later, elated by his achievement. As we began our descent, the rooster probably realized there were to be no bones to chew today, so he went his own way.

My legs were shaking like jelly on a plate, and I seriously wondered whether I would actually make it to the base of the volcano without help from a team of paramedics. Fortunately, I made it down without incident, but painfully I discovered that climbing down is much harder than climbing up. Having reached the foot of the volcano, I was faced with the walk back to where we left the dinghy. There were no taxicabs waiting at the foot of the Quill, which annoyed me. So we walked and walked and walked and walked and walked, with me, like peg leg, limping sadly along behind Bob.

By some magnificent stroke of luck, we stumbled across a little Spanish bar, which appeared before us like a mirage in the desert. We found a seat at a table under the shade of a flamboyant tree (not in bloom), and Bob ordered us a couple of ice-cold beers. Oh, the nectar that is an ice-cold beer on a stifling hot afternoon. After that brief rest, we started out once again: I felt mildly refreshed but was still limping badly. It was about another fifteen-minute walk before we came across the Gin House, a seafront bar where we stopped for another couple of beers. My dark mood was lifting rapidly, the trek was getting better, and I was actually beginning to think that I could make it all the way back to *Whoops-a-Daisy* now. Oh, it's lovely how alcohol confuses the brain and dulls the pain.

That night we had a pleasant meal at Blue Bead, although I have to say I found that the limited menu was not very adventurous, especially considering the high prices. But then I reminded myself that we were in the off-season, and prices everywhere throughout the Caribbean are cheaper in the off-season. All in all, however, it must be said the food was fresh and well prepared, the service was warm and friendly, and the views out across the ocean were beautiful.

All good things come to an end, and it was time to return *Daisy* back to the British Virgin Islands.

Leaving *Daisy* and returning to Ohio was bittersweet: I was so excited to be going home and yet sad to be leaving. I was elated at having completed the voyage from Tortola to Aruba and back to St. Maarten. Looking back over the past two years, I realized I had come face-to-face with many of my fears. There were times when I had been filled with joy, terrified out of my mind, and humbled by Mother Nature. I had survived a hurricane, conquered my fear of deep water, swam with sharks, hiked up volcanoes; the list goes on and on—so many experiences I had never dreamed of. Now I was heading back to civilization and life ashore for a few weeks, maybe months. I wondered how I would fare back in the real world where I would be bombarded with traffic jams, taxes, and Twitter.

It turns out that I wasn't as keen to leave *Daisy* as I thought I would be. Perhaps people *can* change. After all, I was already dreaming about our next adventure. Who would have thought!

Captain Bob and First mate Heather aka Long Jane Silver! (me thinks, taken perhaps after a cocktail or two!)

Appendix 1:
Traveling Abroad with Pets

Traveling abroad with pets is no picnic. Aside from dealing with the poor, terrified creature, there's a mountain of documentation and requirements to be met before you travel. Start this process at least three months prior to your intended departure date.

Once you've made the decision to travel with your pet, you need to be absolutely sure that you have all the required paperwork, permissions, shots, health certificates, etc., in order, or the authorities will confiscate your pet. Having traveled many times now with my cat, Nicho-San, I can offer some advice.

The very first thing you'll want to do is keep a folder handy to file all your pet's paperwork.

Step 1: Obtain a titer. This can take up to three months, so make sure you allow plenty of time. Your veterinarian takes a blood sample from your pet and sends it to a special laboratory for testing. The lab then sends the titer document back to the veterinarian, who will provide you with a copy.

Note: Make sure you obtain the original document and have your vet keep the copy. Some countries insist on seeing the original. Check with your veterinarian regarding the cost to do this.

Step 2: Get your pet microchipped. Your veterinarian injects the microchip into the flabby skin at the back of the neck, a painless procedure for your pet. The microchip traces lost pets by satellite. Keep the certificate with the microchip number in your folder with the rest of your pet's paperwork.

Step 3: For each country you're flying to, find out exact requirements for the importation of pets. Different countries have different requirements, so check with each country's department of agriculture. Not all countries require the same shots.

Gather a list of required shots, and have your veterinarian administer them to your pet. Keep a complete immunization record confirming the dates the shots were completed.

Step 4: Get a health certificate signed by an accredited veterinarian (one approved by the department of agriculture for the country you are visiting). *Note: Not all vets are accredited, so check this.*

Step 5: Get your health certificate approved. Make an appointment at the nearest U.S. or U.K. department of agriculture office to get the health certificate approved.

The department will want to see *all* of your paperwork and records, so take everything with you: titer, microchip, and shot record. Once the department has checked and approved your paperwork, they will sign the health certificate and return it to you. Unless there is a problem, this will be done the same day; the entire procedure usually takes less than one hour. A fee may be required.

Step 6: Contact the department of agriculture for the country you're flying into and advise them of your intention to import a pet. They might ask you to fax them copies of all your pet's paperwork as well as your travel and flight information.

The country you're flying into may possibly send a representative to meet you at the airport to check all your paperwork. Make copies of all the important documents to give them. This is not required, but I've always found that they appreciate this.

Here are more helpful tips:

Always keep the documentation with the pet; don't pack it into checked luggage. If your luggage gets lost and you don't have the documentation on hand when you arrive, the authorities will confiscate your pet.

Check with the airline to make sure there is space for your pet on the plane if the pet is traveling on board with you. Most airlines only allow two or three pets on each flight and usually charge about $100 per flight per pet. Some airlines do not allow any pets to travel on board, so it's important that you check this out well in advance. You also should check to make sure there is space if your pet will be traveling in a crate below the plane.

If you're bringing your pet on board, make sure you have a carrier that will fit under the airline seat.

Ask your vet for some tranquilizer tablets to carry with you in case of an emergency.

Take a collapsible water holder and a small bag of your pet's regular food.

Bring a harness for both cats and dogs. You will be required to remove your pet from its traveling cage in order to go through the security screening. Trying to hold on to a terrified cat is no easy matter, and it's no fun chasing it through a busy airport.

If you intend to live on board with your pet, I highly recommend the book *Cruising With Your Four-Footed Friends* by Diana Jessie.

Happy travels.

Appendix 2:

Galley Notes

I'm a passionate cook who's never happier than when in the kitchen making delicious dishes for my family and friends or creating new recipes. When I moved from my home to a sailboat, going overnight from my beautiful, professionally equipped kitchen to a galley the size of a shoebox, I found myself confronted with some major challenges.

One thing I struggled with was shopping for groceries and fresh ingredients, and then keeping those ingredients fresh (everything goes bad in a couple of days in the Caribbean humidity). The selection available to the consumer can be quite limited.

When you're on vacation, you don't want to spend hours and hours in a sweltering hot galley, sweating buckets over a hot stove. At the same time, you do want to eat well. And a fabulous restaurant may not always be right there on the beach where you happened to have dropped anchor for the night, so it pays to be prepared.

After almost ten years of chartering and five years of living aboard, I've adapted and learned a few tricks to help create easy, quick, and delicious meals.

I thought long and hard about the recipes to include in this book. There are many wonderful cookbooks out there, and I didn't want to publish just another cookbook. This was to be mainly a travel journal, after all, but I wanted to include some of my favorite dishes that can be quickly prepared on board, using ingredients easily found in the Caribbean. I hope that the few recipes and tips I've included in this book will make your time aboard a little easier, whether you're vacationing or living on board full-time.

Things I wouldn't dream of doing in my home kitchen are normal practice on board. I found these changes necessary to make life in the galley easier and meal preparation faster. I've changed my recipes to suit the conditions. For example, I take shortcuts: I buy ready-made pasta, pastries, and bread instead of making my own.

The high humidity in the Caribbean causes so many problems with baking, and cooking time really needs to be limited because you'll most likely be using bottled gas. That's why I've chosen recipes with ingredients that are easily found, and, with only the odd exception, the preparation and cooking times are relatively quick.

Here is a list of items I always keep stocked in *Daisy*'s galley, as well as tips on how to store them.

I like to use **Maldon sea salt flakes**; this is a personal choice. Maldon salt doesn't contain all the chemicals and additives that are found in many table salts; it's just pure flaked sea salt. You may need to bring it with you from the mainland, because it's not easily found in the Caribbean. A good alternative would be **coarse sea salt** or **kosher salt.**

I also bring **dried herbs** from the mainland. Jars and bottles of herbs and spices often sit on shelves for a very long time in the Caribbean, and you also have to consider the heat they're exposed to. At home I use fresh herbs, but they're often not easily found in the Caribbean (other than in Grenada). Don't keep opened dried herbs longer than twelve months; they quickly lose their flavor.

I always keep a good selection of dried mushrooms on board, particularly **morel** and **porcini.** Fresh mushrooms only keep a day or two at the most, unless you have really good airtight containers.

I always keep several oils on board. I like the fruitier, greener **extra-virgin olive oils** from Southern Italy. I use them for dressings and light sautéing. Always store them in a cool dark place. **Peanut oil** is great for light sautéing and stir-frying. **Walnut oil** has a high smoke point of 400 degrees, so it's good for baking and frying. And **Canola oil**, which is monounsaturated, is great for deep-frying.

Vegetables that keep well on board for two to three weeks are butternut squash, onions, potatoes, yucca, cassava, and green and red cabbage. Always try and buy under-ripe **fruit**, because it ripens very quickly in the heat. Granny Smith apples last the longest. Melons, pineapples, plantains, and bananas will keep for at least a couple of days, longer if unripe. But they can go bad overnight, and if you don't get rid of them, your boat will fill with fruit flies.

Keep fruits and vegetables in a hammock in an airy place, or in a canvas or hessian bag. Don't ever store anything fresh in plastic bags. Plastic causes organic matter to sweat and then go moldy. Airtight containers are invaluable for tomatoes and mushrooms.

Pasta, rice, flour, sugar, biscuits, and crackers should always be stored in well- sealed, airtight containers to keep insects out.

Always buy **long-life milk, cream, and juices**; it is surprising how quickly fresh can turn bad.

I always keep **a few containers of firm tofu** on board. It's really versatile and keeps a long time in the fridge if unopened. Tofu is a great substitute for meat when supplies run low.

Here are a few more food storage tips:

Take the time to **plan each individual meal**, remembering how many people you are catering for. This will help you provision efficiently, and you will waste less. Plan your meals so you use the most perishable items first.

Don't ever take cardboard boxes on board. They may contain cockroaches or other unwanted insects, and once they're on board, you'll almost certainly never get rid of them.

When buying food for the freezer, if possible **always buy food that is already frozen**. Boat freezers are often not as efficient as home freezers and take a very long time to freeze fresh food. Also, adding unfrozen food uses a lot of extra power. Putting unfrozen food in a freezer will raise the freezer temperature and defrost the other food stored in there.

Appendix 3:
Preparing Fresh Whole Fish

The tools required to successfully clean and debone fresh fish:

* A sharp filleting knife
* A large, sharp knife
* A fish scaler (although you could use the back of a knife).
* A set of needle-nose pliers, or a pair of tweezers
* Heavy-duty kitchen scissors

For preparation purposes, divide fish into two types, "round" and "flat". Rounder-bodied fish, such as sea bass and salmon, and flat fish, such as sole and place.

To prepare a round fish:

Start by removing the fins with scissors.

Remove the head by cutting at an angle on each side behind the gills, then under the fin on the underside with the sharp knife, and snap off the head. (the head can be saved and used for stock)

Hold the fish by its tail and scrape away from you using the fish scaler, (the back of a knife). This lifts and removes the scales.

Trim the tail into a neat V-shape, or remove it completely, with the kitchen scissors.

Lay the fish on one side, press down with your hand flat on the top side, then using the heavy duty knife parallel to the fish, slice the fish along its belly from tail to head, being careful not to cut too deep and pierce the intestines, (they have bitter acids that could spoil the flavor of the fish)

Remove the intestines, pull them all out with your fingers. There will also be a small white sack by the backbone, this is the kidney, remove it with the knife.

Wash the inside of the fish thoroughly, wiping with kitchen paper towels to remove any left over bits of blood or membrane.

The fish is now ready to either prepare for cooking whole, or filleting.

To fillet a whole fresh fish:

Make an incision along the back of the fish, one side of the dorsal fin, as if beginning to cleave the fish into its two halves.

Place the tip of the knife inside the cut, and run the knife from head to tail along the bones. Keep the bottom of the blade tight against the bones so that these bones are separated from the fillet.

Make long, even strokes. Do not saw back and forth or you will destroy the fillets. Use a sharp blade, and keep the knife flat, this will produce neater fillets (they will also keep their shape better during cooking.) hold the fillet in your hand and snip it loose at the tail. Trim any loose skin around the fillet to tidy it.

With the filleting knife slice under any rib bones and pull out with your fingers. Use the tweezers to remove any tiny bones, you will find these by running your finger tips from head to toe gently massaging to locate their sharp points, the bones typically run down the center of the fillet.

To skin a fillet:

Place the fish skin-side down on the cutting board.

Hold the tail flap of the fillet with one hand, and with the knife held at a slight angle so its almost flat with the board, begin approximately one quarter of an inch from the tail end and cut between the skin and the flesh, gently pull the tail with your hand as you saw gently forward with the knife, separating the skin from the flesh.

If your knife is sharp and your hold firm, the skin should cut fairly easily from the flesh.

Appendix 4:
Helpful Websites

Cooper Island:	www.cooperisland.com
Virgin Gorda:	www.bvitourism.com/virgin-gorda
Bitter End:	www.beyc.com
Braveheart Charters, Jerry Blair:	www.braveheartcharters.com
Montserrat:	www.visitmonsterrat.com,
	www.lonelyplanet.com/monsterrat
Montserrat Volcano Activity:	www.mvo.com
St. Eustatius:	www.statiatourism.com,
	www.lonelyplanet.com/sint-eustatius
St. Kitts:	www.stkittstourism.kn/explore,
	www.lonelyplanet.com/st-kitts-and-nevis
Nevis:	www.nevisisland.com/
Four Seasons, Nevis:	www.fourseasons.com/nevis
Young Island:	www.youngisland.com,
	www.youngislandresorts.com
Mustique:	www.mustique-island.com,
	www.mustique.com
Dominica:	www.dominica.dm,
	www.lonelyplanet.com/dominica
Guadeloupe:	www.lonelyplanet.com/guadeloupe

Tobago Cays: www.tobagocays.com/
Grenada: www.grenadagrenadines.com/
Le Phare Bleu Boutique Hotel,
Marina and Resort: www.lepharebleu.com

Le Phare Bleu onsite services:
The Canvas Shop at Le Phare Bleu Grenada, Jane and Dave Royce, thecanvass-hop@spiceisle.com; tel (473) 443 2960, cell (473) 449 0780

Palm Tree Marine Ltd, Mike Bingley at Le Phare Bleu
Marine and electrical engineers, fuel polishing and tank cleaning
mike@palmtreemarine.com, www.palmtreemarine.com; tel (473) 443 2960, cell (473) 449 0780

Los Roques: www.losroques.org/
Bonaire: www.infobonaire.com/,
                                  www.lonelyplanet.com/aruba-bonaire-and-curacao/bonaire
Aruba: www.aruba.com/

Submarine rides in Aruba: www.atlantisadventures.com/aruba/atlantis-submarine-expedition/
Curacao: www.curacao.com/
St. Maarten/St. Martin: www.st-maarten.com,
                                  www.gorgraphia.com/st-martin/,
                                  www.lonelyplanet.com/st-martin-sint-maarten

Appendix 5:
Glossary of Basic Boating Terms

aboard. On or within the boat.

above deck. On the boat deck.

adrift. Loose, not on moorings or towline.

aft. Toward the stern of the boat.

aground. Touching or fast to the bottom.

anchor. A heavy metal device, fastened to a chain or a line, that holds a vessel in position, partly because of its weight, but chiefly because of its shape, which is designed to dig into the bottom.

anchorage. A place suitable for anchoring in relation to the wind, seas, and bottom.

aweigh. The position of the anchor as it's raised clear of the bottom.

batten down. To secure hatches and loose objects both within the hull and on the deck.

beam. The greatest width of the boat.

bearing. The direction of an object expressed either as a true bearing as shown on the chart, or as a bearing relative to the heading of the boat.

below. Beneath the deck.

bilge. The interior of the hull below the floorboards.

bimini. A canvas canopy over the cockpit and helm.

bitter end. The last part of a rope or chain; the inboard end of the anchor rope.

boat hook. A short shaft with a fitting at one end shaped to facilitate putting a line over a piling, recovering an object dropped overboard, or pushing or fending off.

bosun's locker. A storage space in a boat's fore deck, usually used for storing sails and fenders.

bow. The forward part of a boat.

bowline. A docking line leading from the bow.

bowline knot. A knot used to form a temporary loop in the end of a line.

bow spring line. A bow pivot line used in docking and undocking, or to prevent the boat from moving forward or astern while made fast to a pier.

brow. The device used to allow passage of personnel between the shore and a ship. See also **gangplank** or **gangway**.

bulkhead. A vertical partition that separates compartments.

buoy. An anchored float used for mooring or for marking a position on the water, a hazard, or a shoal.**cabin.** A compartment for passengers or crew.

capsize. To turn over.

cast off. To let go.

catamaran. A twin-hulled boat, with hulls side-by-side.

chafing gear. Tubing or cloth wrapping used to protect a line from chafing on a rough surface.

chart. A navigator's map.

cockpit. An opening in the deck from which the boat is handled.

companionway. The entrance into a sailboat's interior.

compass. A navigation instrument, either magnetic (showing magnetic north) or gyro (showing true north).

course. The direction in which a boat is steered.

current. The horizontal movement of water.

day beacon. A fixed navigation aid structure used in shallow waters upon which is placed one or more day marks.

dead ahead. Directly ahead.

dead astern. Directly aft.

deck. A permanent covering over a compartment or a hull, or any part thereof.

dinghy. A small open boat, often used as a tender for a larger craft.

displacement. The weight of water displaced by a floating vessel; thus, a boat's weight.

dock. A protected water area in which vessels are moored. Also, a pier or a wharf.

dodger. A frame-supported canvas over a boat's companionway.

draft. The depth of water a boat draws.

ease. To slacken or relieve tension on a line.

ebb. A receding current.

ebb tide. A receding tide.

even keeled. When a boat is floating on its designed waterline.

eye of the wind. The direction from which the wind is blowing.

fathom. A unit of length equal to six feet, used for measuring the depth of water.

fender. An inflatable cushion that is placed between boats or between a boat and a pier to prevent damage.

flare. A distress signal.

floorboards. The surface of the cockpit on which the crew stands.

forward. Toward the bow of the boat.

galley. The kitchen area of a boat.

gangplank. A moveable bridge used in boarding or leaving a ship at a pier.

gangway. The area of a ship's side where people board and disembark.

gear. A general term for ropes, blocks, tackle, and other equipment.

grab rails. Handhold fittings mounted on cabin tops and sides for personal safety.

ground tackle. A collective term for the anchor and its associated gear.

harbor. A safe anchorage, protected from most storms; may be natural or manmade, with breakwaters and jetties; a place for docking and loading.

hatch. An opening in a boat's deck fitted with a watertight cover.

head. A marine toilet. Also, the upper corner of a triangular sail.

heading. The direction in which a vessel's bow points at any given time.

headway. The forward motion of a boat; opposite of sternway.

heave to. To bring a vessel up in a position where it will maintain little or no headway, usually with the bow into the wind or nearly so.

heel. To tip to one side.

helm. The wheel or tiller controlling the rudder.

helmsperson. The person who steers the boat.

hold. A large vessel's compartment below deck, used solely for carrying cargo.

hull. The main body of a vessel.

jibe. Change of course by swinging a fore-and-aft sail across a following wind.

An **accidental jibe** happens when the boat is steered or the wind shifts such that the stern of the boat accidentally passes through the eye of the wind. This causes the main boom to swing violently to the other side of the boat.

keel. The centerline of a boat running fore and aft; the backbone of a vessel.

knot. A measure of speed equal to one nautical mile (6,076 feet) per hour. To convert knots to statute mph, multiply by 1.14.

latitude. The distance north or south of the equator measured and expressed in degrees.

lazarette. A storage space in a boat's stern area.

lee. The side sheltered from the wind.

leeward. The direction away from the wind; opposite of windward.

leeway. The sideways movement of the boat caused by either wind or current.

line. A rope and cordage used aboard a vessel.

log. A record of courses or operation. Also, a device that measures speed.

longitude. The distance in degrees east or west of the meridian at Greenwich, England.

mast. A spar set upright to support rigging and sails.

midship. A section midway between the bow and the stern.

monohull. A boat with one hull.

mooring. An arrangement for securing a boat to a mooring buoy or a pier.

mooring buoy. A buoy secured to a permanent anchor sunk deep into the bottom.

nautical mile. One minute of latitude; a measurement used in salt water approximately 6,076 feet, about one-eighth longer than the statute mile of 5,280 feet.

navigation. The art and science of conducting a boat safely from one point to another.

navigation rules. The regulations governing the movement of vessels in relation to each other, generally called steering and sailing rules.

outboard. A detachable engine mounted on a boat's stern.

overboard. Over the side or out of the boat.

painter. A line attached to the bow of a boat for use in towing or making fast.

passarella. A retractable brow often installed on yachts.

pennant. The line by which a boat is made fast to a mooring buoy.

personal flotation device (PFD). A life jacket. When properly used, the PDF will support a person in the water.

pier. A loading platform extending at an angle from the shore.

port. The left side of a boat looking forward. Also, a harbor.

propeller. A rotating device, with two or more blades, that acts as a screw in propelling a vessel.

reef. To bring in the sail, reducing the sail area. Also, a chain of rocks or coral or a ridge of sand at or near the surface of the water.

rigging. The general term for all the lines of a vessel.

rode. The anchor line and/or chain.

roll. The alternating motion of a boat, leaning alternately to port and starboard; the motion of a boat about its fore-and-aft axis.

rope. In general, cordage as it is purchased at the store. When it comes aboard a vessel and is put to use, it becomes line.

rudder. A vertical plate or board for steering a boat.

run. To allow a line to feed freely.

running lights. Lights required to be shown on boats underway between sundown and sunup.

satellite navigation. A form of position-finding using radio transmissions from satellites with sophisticated on-board automatic equipment.

scuppers. Drain holes on deck, in the toe-rail and in bulwarks.

sea anchor. Any device used to reduce a boat's drift before the wind.

seamanship. All the arts and skills of boat handling, ranging from maintaining and repairing to piloting, sail handling, marlinespike (a pointed tool used to separate strands of rope) work, and rigging.

seaworthy. A boat or a boat's gear able to meet the usual sea conditions.

secure. To make fast.

ship. A large seagoing vessel able to carry a "boat" on board.

sloop. A single-masted vessel with working sails (main and jib) set fore and aft.

sounding. A measurement of water depth.

splice. To permanently join two ropes by tucking their strands alternately over and under each other.

spring line. A pivot line used in docking and undocking, or to prevent the boat from moving forward or astern while made fast to a dock.

squall. A sudden violent wind often accompanied by rain.

starboard. The right side of a boat when looking forward.

stern. The after part of the boat.

stern line. A docking line leading from the stern.

stow. To put an item in its proper place.

tackle. A combination of blocks and line to increase mechanical advantage.

tender. A dinghy.

tide. The periodic rise and fall of water level in the oceans.

toe-rail. Runs around the perimeter of the deck, where the deck and hull are joined.

transom. The stern cross-section of a square-sterned boat.

true wind. The actual direction from which the wind is blowing.

underway. Vessel in motion, not moored, at anchor, or aground.

VHF radio. A very high frequency electronic communications and direction-finding system.

wake. Moving waves. Also, a track or path that a boat leaves behind it when moving across the waters.

waterline. A line painted on a hull that shows the point to which a boat sinks when it is properly trimmed.

way. Movement of a vessel through the water, such as headway, sternway, or leeway.

weigh anchor. To bring the anchor up from its holding. See also **aweigh**.

winch. A device used to increase hauling power when raising or trimming sails.

windward. Toward the direction from which the wind is coming.

yacht. A pleasure vessel or boat, either sail or power.

Bibliography

Carwardine, Mark, Eric Hoyt, Ewan Fordyce, and Peter Gill. *A Guide to Whales, Dolphins & Porpoises*. Fog City Press, 1998.

DK Eyewitness Travel: Caribbean. DK Publishing, 1999.

Doyle, Chris. *Cruising Guide, 2002-2003*. Chris Doyle Publishing, 2001.

Doyle, Chris, and Nancy Scott. *2003-2004 Sailors Guide to the Windward Islands*. Chris Doyle Publishing, 2002.

Radila Scott, Carolina. *Insight Guide Caribbean: The Lesser Antilles*. APA Publications UK, Ltd., 2004.

Scott, Nancy, and Simon Scott. *2009-2011 Cruising Guide to the Virgin Islands*. Cruising Guide Publications Inc., 2008.

Sullivan, Lynne M. *Hunter Travel Guide to Grenada, St. Vincent, and the Grenadines*. Hunter Publishing, Inc., 2003.

Waterson, D., and D. van der Reijden. *Gotta Go Cruising: The ABC Islands*. Compass Consultants Ltd., 2006.